BMW MINI

An Enthusiast's Guide

T0306557

BMW MINI

An Enthusiast's Guide

Sophie Williamson-Stothert

THE CROWOOD PRESS

First published in 2016 by
The Crowood Press Ltd
Ramsbury, Marlborough
Wiltshire SN8 2HR

www.crowood.com

© Sophie Williamson-Stothert 2016

All rights reserved. No part of this publication may be
reproduced or transmitted in any form or by any means,
electronic or mechanical, including photocopy, recording, or any
information storage and retrieval system, without permission in
writing from the publishers.

British Library Cataloguing-in-Publication Data
A catalogue record for this book is available from the British
Library.

ISBN 978 1 78500 143 7

Dedication
For Mum and Dad, Rose and Andrew, Guy Loveridge and
Richard Aucock, who, through all their love and support,
have always encouraged me to chase my dreams, including
this very book you hold in your hands.

Illustration Acknowledgements
With thanks to Richard and Vicky Dredge at Magic Car Pics,
www.magiccarpics.co.uk
Unless otherwise stated, photographs are from the author's
collection.

Typeset by Shane O'Dwyer, Swindon, Wiltshire

Printed and bound in India by Replika Press Pvt Ltd

CONTENTS

FOREWORD

The Mini is, without much danger of contradiction, one of the most important motor cars of the 20th century. It was certainly what we now like to refer to as a 'game changer'. When it was introduced in 1959 it revolutionized the motoring scene, and the fact that we still refer to a certain class of cars as 'Mini cars' and 'Super Mini' reveals the length of the shadow cast.

It's pretty easy to see why BMW wanted to capitalize on the strength of 'brand identity' that had grown up around the Mini as a life-style, fashion, motoring and individualistic icon. The trick, of course, was adapting the front-wheel drive, wheel at each corner and 'cute' looks to a 21st-century market-place that demanded far more of their car than the generation who queued up to buy the plethora of Mini variants being produced at Cowley and Longbridge five decades before.

My 'Mini motoring' has covered ownership of a few of the more esoteric variations upon the theme. In the 1990s when I was a jobbing actor and landed my first part in a West End run, I would commute in a 1965 Riley Elf – the ideal car for such a job, and I've owned another identical one since. Then as the Mini's 50th anniversary approached I combined two interests and became the proud owner of the actual Deep Sanderson 301 that Chris Lawrence took to Le Mans in 1963 and 1964, thus becoming the first Mini-based car to compete at La Sarthe in the legendary 24 Hours race. This machine I drove at Goodwood in the Festival of Speed and then again for the 2009 tribute parade for the Birthday, following Mr Bean around on the roof of his Mini City.

The car went on to race at The Goodwood Revival and acquitted itself amazingly well in such exalted company, with a top 10 finish only being wrenched from its fingers by a recovering competitor who was four laps down and did not understand Blue Flags! The 'Deepers' went on to return to Le Mans in the Classic of 2014, acquitting itself pretty well.

I now have a 1962 Ogle SX 1000, which I repatriated from the USA and am restoring to original specification, complete with 998cc Cooper engine as per its original options list. So, I think it is fair to say, I am steeped in Minis and their ways....

When Sophie told me she was writing this book, I was a little surprised, as I checked my bookshelf and saw over twenty-five titles all concerned with Minis, but having now read it, I am mightily impressed as she has succeeded in explaining the links, the ethos and the brave attempt to engender a 'reborn' BMW-sired Mini and to steer the brand in a completely new and enhanced direction. That the 21st Century Mini is a success will doubtless be reflected in the popularity of this first class book. Enjoy. I did.

GUY LOVERIDGE
Chairman – The Guild of Motoring Writers
July 2015

THE Mini/MINI STORY, 1959 TO 2015

Sophie with her R50 MINI Cooper at Plant Oxford.
JAMES BATCHELOR

Manufactured by the British Motor Corporation (BMC), British Leyland (BL) and Rover Group between 1959 and the year 2000, the classic Mini was moulded into a line of iconic British small cars. During those forty-one years, these firms produced the Morris Mini-Minor, the Austin Se7en, the Mini Countryman, the army service Mini Moke, the Mini Clubman and more. The little Mini wasn't denied any horsepower either, and when performance Cooper versions of these models were modified in partnership with racing legend John Cooper, the little car – designed to provide transportation for families – became a rally legend: three times. In 1959, the small car was launched as the Morris Mini-Minor and the Austin Se7en (A7). In 1961 it was renamed Austin Mini, and eight years later, in 1969 – ten years after the first Mini rolled off the production line – the Mini became a marque in its own right. The original Mini revolutionized the small car and became the best-selling British car in history. It continued to roll off the production line until the very end of its era in the year 2000, selling 5.3 million units. Its legacy was continued when in 1995, the development stages of its successor – the R-Series MINI – began.

Since its launch in 2001, BMW's modern MINI has become the pinnacle of small yet funky family cars in the premium small car segment – although many may argue that the modern MINI is far too large to be branded such a title. In keeping with a similar theme to that of the 1960s and 1970s, the MINI range has followed in the footsteps of its predecessor's line-up, with a few extra additions. Now in its third generation,

LEFT: **1964 RAC Rally and 1965 Monte Carlo Mini Cooper S.** GUY LOVERIDGE

BELOW: **The first generation R50 MINI line-up: One, Cooper and Cooper S.** NEWSPRESS

having unveiled the new F-Series in 2014, BMW MINI offers the hatchback, the Convertible, the estate Clubman, the five-door Countryman, the Coupé, the Roadster and the three-door crossover Paceman. Like the classic Mini, a number of these models are available with the John Cooper Works performance pack and have been released in special editions such as the Mayfair and the London 2012 – providing a little something for everyone.

PART I

WHERE IT
ALL BEGAN

CHAPTER ONE

BMC'S MINI

The Mini was originally a product of the British Motor Corporation (BMC), which later became a part of British Motor Holdings (BMH) in 1966, and eventually merged with Leyland Motors in 1968 to form British Leyland. It wasn't until 1969 (ten years after its birth) that Mini became an automotive marque in its own right. During the late 1980s, British Leyland was demolished and Mini joined Rover Group. In 1994, Rover Group was acquired by BMW, which the brand later dissolved in 2000, while retaining the Mini/MINI brand. Today, the MINI division is led by Sebastian Mackensen.

It took just one man to design the ultimate small family car, the very machine that, thanks to its transverse-engine, front-wheel-drive layout, is capable of seating four adults, has a luggage compartment (albeit small) and the ability to bring a smile to each and every one of its drivers' faces. Little did he know that this little car would go on to become an iconic symbol of British heritage: the Mini was a motoring legend both on the road and on the race circuit.

Britain's small car was born in response to an economic and political crisis, and it soon became a little car that gave mobility to millions. Sir Alec Issigonis's baby was created in response to the Middle East crisis when, in September 1956, Colonel Nasser decided to nationalize the Suez Canal and use the Arabs' control of the world's oil supplies to hold the rest of the word to ransom. When the Arabs closed their

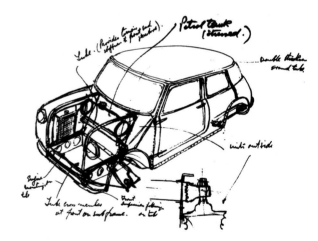

ABOVE: **Original sketch of the Mini prototype by Alec Issigonis in 1958.** NEWSPRESS

LEFT: **A bird's-eye sketch of the Mini 850, by Alec Issigonis in 1958.** MAGIC CAR PICS

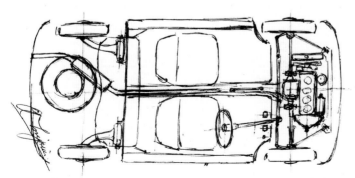

oil pipeline across the Mediterranean, in the ensuing war they blew up the Syrian pipeline that provided 20 per cent of Britain's petrol supply. This resulted in petrol rationing hitting the UK in December that year, and inevitably, a newly found popularity for small cars across Europe.

In the period between 1956 and 1957, the sales of 900 to 1000cc cars rocketed. This explains the appearance of German bubble cars in the UK, which could achieve more than 40 miles per gallon (7ltr/100km) – the ideal statistic for families living in a petrol-starved period. At the end of 1955, Leonard Lord invited Issigonis to rejoin BMC after three years at Alvis Motors. Lord Leonard quite frankly despised bubble cars, and is reported to have said to Issigonis in March 1957: 'God damn these bloody awful bubble cars. We must drive them off the streets by designing a proper small car.' From that point, BMC's new car development programme changed from replacing the Morris Minor to producing a new small car.

An engineering team of four draftsmen, a group of student engineers and three talented men, including Chris Kingham from Alvis Motors, Jack Daniels who helped produce the Minor, John Sheppard who was responsible for the design, and Issigonis himself, set about designing and defining the Mini – the XC9003, which later became project ADO15 when development moved to the Austin HQ at Longbridge. Issigonis saw front-wheel drive as the powertrain for his future cars, and ADO15 would become the first practical four-seater crammed into a small package to reach production.

Up until 2015, John Sheppard was the last surviving member of the classic Mini design team. Under the direction of Issigonis, he led the construction of BMC's revolutionary car in the late 1950s. Sheppard was largely responsible for the structure of the body, as well as the Mini's many cost-saving features. Essentially, he was there to translate Issigonis's scribbles into more credible designs. Every cost-saving feature, including the little car's door bins, which were large enough to hold gin and vermouth bottles to mix Issigonis a dry Martini, were designed by Sheppard. But he didn't always have the final say when it came to making official decisions: in one difference of opinion he lost an argument with Issigonis over the construction of the floor, and was forced to draw up a design that he knew would leak. To put into perspective just how much water the little Minis originally took on board, one road-test journalist returned from an outing with a goldfish lodged in one of those signature door pockets. To combat the floor-leaking issue, every Mini was supplied with a pair of Wellington boots as standard. Thankfully, that wasn't the only resolution, and eventually Sheppard was given authority to redesign the underbody of the Mini to stop the water gushing in, just as he had originally intended.

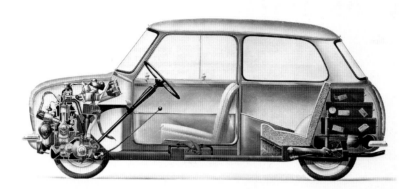

The longitudinal section of the Morris Mini-Minor and Austin Se7en 1959. NEWSPRESS

Issigonis had already proved with his work on the Morris Minor replacement that he could fit an engine and gearbox into a space of just 2 feet (60cm) of a car's entire length. But when the Mini was destined to be a narrow vehicle, it was difficult to see how the package would be accommodated between the Mini's wheels without compromising the steering lock. The first attempt at resolving this problem was for an A-Series engine to lose two cylinders, creating an in-line, 2-cylinder, 500cc engine. As would be expected, the engine lacked 'oomph' and was far too rough for the job. Issigonis resolved the issue by mounting the gearbox underneath the engine, as part of an in-sump arrangement – a crucial part of the first Mini mock-up. By July, just four months after the development began, the first prototype was up and running. ADO15 used a conventional BMC A-Series,

4-cylinder, water-cooled engine. The Mini's space-saving transverse-engine, front-wheel-drive layout meant that 80 per cent of the car's floorpan could be used to seat passengers and store luggage, therefore influencing a generation of car makers.

Weight and length were critical in the development of the Mini. The fact that the first prototype was 6mm (¼in) over 3m (10ft) long irritated Issigonis immensely. The team were eventually able to make the Mini 45kg (100lb) lighter than the Austin A35, which would inevitably become a key factor in ensuring that the car retained competitive fuel consumption figures, which would later prove difficult to beat for the likes of British Leyland. It is rumoured that in July 1957 the BMC chairman Leonard Lord first drove the prototype around the Longbridge plant, instructing Issigonis to 'build the bloody thing'. A second

Front axle and engine of the Morris Mini-Minor and Austin Se7en 1959. NEWSPRESS

ADO15 used a conventional BMC A-Series, 4-cylinder, water-cooled engine. MAGIC CAR PICS

ABOVE: **Many were unsure as to why Issigonis pushed the development of 10-inch wheels.** MAGIC CAR PICS

RIGHT: **The Mini featured a basic but revolutionary interior with space for four adults.** MAGIC CAR PICS

prototype was soon born. Both cars were disguised with Austin A35 grilles and based at Cowley in the hands of engineers from Morris Motors, who would later play a significant role in the development of all the front-wheel-drive cars to follow in the footsteps of the Mini.

Although the little Minis shared a number of design weaknesses and would later undergo a range of engineering tweaks, the Mini was finally on its way to production. A big question mark hovered above the Mini's minute 10in wheels for a long period of time. Most people couldn't understand the purpose in creating a smaller road wheel, but Issigonis pushed the development of the small car by working with Dunlop to produce the smallest road tyre. The industry average rim size at the time sat at 16–17in. Nonetheless, the Mini needed small tyres to optimize cabin space. Dunlop eventually produced 5.20in tyres that appeared on the Mini.

Joint managing director of BMC George Harriman teased journalists about the small car that would provide drivers with a low-priced, fully engineered car to replace the Germans' bubble cars. By March 1958 the first two prototypes had driven 50,000 miles (80,000km), and the decision was made to build ten pilot production cars. The ADO15 Mini was turning out to be a difficult design to drive into production,

and George Harriman wasn't impressed by the little car's appearance, referring to it as 'what a bloody mess'. But soon, many would beg to differ.

By November 1959, Mini production had taken the world by storm. BMC announced a £49m expansion plan, with a plan to double output to 8,000 Minis per week. By the end of the year, 19,749 Minis had been built and delivered to happy owners. The Mini was arguably one of the most awkward vehicles to piece together, not because of its fiddly parts or unique design, but because BMC had so many manufacturing plants spread out across the country. The A-Series engine was built at Moors Engines at Courthouse Green in Coventry, the front-wheel-drive gearbox came from both Longbridge and Drews Lane in Birmingham, while body pressings came from the Fisher and Ludlow plant at Llanelli in Wales. The components destined to reach Cowley had to be transported from the plants to Oxford, while the body pressings were taken to the Fisher and Ludlow plant at Castle Bromwich for assembly into bodyshells.

The question was whether or not the Mini was actually making or losing BMC money. These days, it is difficult to imagine picking up a brand new state-of-the-art family car for £496.95 – the price for the base model of the world's most advanced family car; even for 1959, that was considerably low for an advanced family vehicle. Some say that Austin's prices mirrored what William Morris (of Morris Motors Limited) charged in the era before BMC; Leonard Lord of Austin believed that William Morris was the master of cost control and assumed that Longbridge-built cars cost a similar price to manufacture as they did to sell. With the formation of BMC, the corporation decided to price the little Mini at a similar figure to the Ford Popular, which also ceased production in 1959.

According to Terry Beckett – Ford UK's senior product planner who went on to become chairman of Ford Britain – Ford calculated that BMC was actually losing £30 on every Mini to leave the production line. As Minis were selling like cupcakes by this point, it is unlikely that raising the price by an extra £30 would have damaged its sales appeal. Nevertheless, BMW stood firm at providing more for less.

THE POWER OF THE MINI

When the first Mini – a Morris Mini-Minor – was sold in 1959, not even its creator knew what impact it would have on motorists' lives. This car, possibly the smallest thing on four wheels, would become so much more than a car. Since the car was marketed under BMC's two main brand names, Austin and

Morris, the Mini was launched in the form of the Morris Mini-Minor and the Austin Se7en, which were essentially the same car. The two distinctively branded cars were launched with the 848cc A-Series engine, and were available in the Basic base model priced at £497 (which didn't get buyers a heater) or the De Luxe at £537. The Morris Mini-Minor also added a Super De Luxe variant for an extra £24, or the De Luxe Automatic, which was £606 at launch. The thing is, this Mini was personalized by its designer in that the car didn't feature a seatbelt or a radio, because Issigonis didn't wear a seatbelt or listen to the radio when he was driving, and similarly, because he smoked like a chimney, an ashtray was incorporated into the Mini's design. In fact, it is thanks to the Mini that the 'bus driver' phrase was born; this is because the Mini featured upright seats that were bolted into one position, and even the later Issigonis cars and the Metro of the 1980s were equipped with these.

The official launch day was 26 August 1969, the same day that the Austin 35 went out of production – the car that the Mini was essentially replacing. The Mini was even quicker to build than the A35, with engineers at the Longbridge and Cowley plants able to produce them at a rate of thirty cars per hour. But because BMC had separate dealerships for its component companies, there were variants of

The first Mini – a Morris Mini-Minor – was launched in 1959. MAGIC CAR PICS

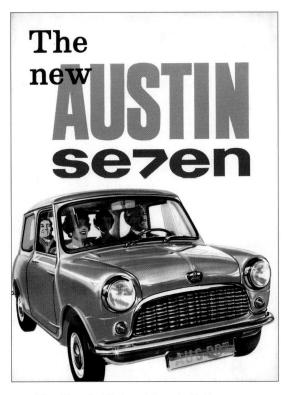

The Morris Mini and Austin Se7en were launched on 26 August 1959. MAGIC CAR PICS

By the early 1960s, the Mini was the UK's most popular small car. MAGIC CAR PICS

ADO15 available – the Austin Se7en and the Morris Mini-Minor. The initial production target was for the Longbridge and Cowley plants to hit 3,000 vehicles per week, with the Fisher and Ludlow plant producing 4,000; by this point, more than 2,000 examples of the Mini had already been shipped abroad and displayed in almost a hundred countries.

The launch of the Mini outshined that of Ford's new Anglia 105E, and, sadly for Ford, both cars were aimed at the same buyers. The Mini even came with a cheaper price tag than the Anglia, which cost £93 more. Adding to its success, the Mini also overtook the Morris Minor as the corporation's bestseller in its first year of production. But it wasn't all plain sailing for the little Mini. Leonard Lord had designed the Mini for typical customers, outgoing families looking for a spacious, practical car. Many drivers considered size to be equal to status, making the Mini look rather off-putting to its target audience, and driving them to buy the larger and, arguably, simpler Ford 100E

Popular or the Austin A40. But what they didn't realize was that the Mini was in fact a very cleverly packaged family car, and benefited from being much smoother and sharper to drive than its Ford rival.

But the Mini was far from perfect. It had a number of teething problems, which prevented sales from rocketing during the early days – though funnily enough, it is those technical glitches that make the Mini so 'adorable' today. When we're out on the open road we all expect to lose oil pressure, overheat, snap a distributor or need a set of new plugs along the way. The Mini actually suffered from internal oil leaks that would often drench the clutch plates, and would often come to a spluttering halt in stormy showers due to the distributor and spark plugs being exposed to the elements at the front of the engine. Its floor-mounted starter switch also played up during showers. It is no wonder the early buyers were a little unsure, dismayed by BMC's engineering choices behind the Mini. Nevertheless the

ABOVE: **The Mini overtook the Morris Minor as BMC's bestseller in its first year of production.** MAGIC CAR PICS

RIGHT: **Mini owners wanted only the best for their little cars, supported by BMC.** MAGIC CAR PICS

Mini was an attractive little motor and, deep down, the British wanted to see it pass beyond its faults and live up to the expectation set by its creator – and so it did.

In January 1960 the Mini Van and Mini estate cars were born, and 800 workers began working a night shift at Cowley Plant to boost Mini production. BMC announced the Morris Mini-Traveller (also released as the Austin Se7en Countryman) and the Austin Se7en Van (also released as the Morris Mini Van), with both the Countryman and Traveller featuring BMC's signature wooden frame for decorative purposes. The Austin Countryman, Morris Traveller and Mini Van had an increased wheelbase of more than 9cm (4in) over the saloon, increasing the overall length by 22cm (10in), and double swinging doors at the rear.

Through all its faults, the Mini lived up to the expectations set by its creator. MAGIC CAR PICS

THE STORY BEHIND A BRITISH AUTOMOTIVE LANDMARK

Mini Plant Oxford is the Great British manufacturing landmark where iconic cars have been built for generations. It tells the romantic tale of the birth of many of the UK's most successful cars. It is where William Morris designed the Morris Minor, and where thousands of engineers welded endless sheets of metal in order to build them – the production lines weren't run by robotic machines, they were run and managed by hundreds of hardworking men and women, with plenty of elbow grease. Moving into the twenty-first century, Plant Oxford – now named Oxford MINI – is of course where the Mini was reinvented as MINI: the reincarnation of Britain's all-time favourite car. By 2002, more than 100,000 MINIs had rolled off the production line since 2001. The Cowley Plant celebrated a century of vehicle production in 2013.

ABOVE: **MINI celebrated a century of vehicle production at Plant Oxford in 2013.** NEWSPRESS

BELOW: **Plant Oxford celebrates the 100,000th MINI rolling off the production line in 2002.** NEWSPRESS

In January 1960, the Morris Mini Van and Austin
Se7en Van were born. NEWSPRESS

BMC later launched the Morris Mini-Traveller
and Austin Se7en Countryman. NEWSPRESS

The Morris Mini-Traveller and Mini Van stayed
in production until 1967 and 1969. NEWSPRESS

The Traveller and Countryman models featured
BMC's signature wooden frame. MAGIC CAR PICS

Both the Traveller and
Countryman were powered
by the same 848cc engine.
MAGIC CAR PICS

FAR MORE PAYLOAD ROOM IN FAR LESS SPACE

..in a vehicle

UNDER **11ft.** LONG **3·4m**

with

UP TO **50** DELIVERY-MILES PER GALLON **18km** PER LITRE

and

TIME SAVING PERFORMANCE

It's never been achieved before—a van so BIG inside, so COMPACT outside—offering so much payload space for each low cost and upkeep!

Packed with revolutionary engineering ideas, this Morris Mini-Van is planned to cut overheads to the lowest possible figure.

Less than 11 feet (3·4 m.) long, it is supremely manoeuvrable. Its big capacity means fewer journeys, less time wasted in 'turn-rounds', speedier on-and-off loading—a saving of many man-hours every working day!

Here's the opportunity to give a more efficient and profitable service than your competitors. Put the Mini-Van on your strength as soon as you can!

NOW SEE HOW IT'S DONE

The Morris Mini Van would later become available with the 998cc engine. MAGIC CAR PICS

The Morris Mini-Traveller was the Morris-badged version of the Austin; they were both powered by the same 848cc engine as the standard Mini, and had an identical price at £623. The Morris Mini-Traveller and Mini Van stayed in production the longest; the Austin models only reached 1961, but the Traveller remained in production until 1967 – it was also launched in an all-metal version in 1962, priced at £532 – with the Mini Van lasting until 1969. The Austin and Morris Vans were much cheaper at £360, although the Morris Mini Van would later become available with the legendary 998cc engine in 1967.

Weekly production by the end of 1960 stood at 3,300 – a rather healthy figure considering that the recession had just hit the motor trade and BMC were forced to move 23,500 workers on to part-time shifts. In fact at the end of 1960, the Mini was already selling better than the Austin A35 – and was even capturing the attention of the likes of Ford. In one month in 1960 the Mini had achieved a 19 per cent market penetration. Buyers were gradually beginning to realize they could really purchase a small car that was cheap to run and easy to manoeuvre around town, while still providing enough room for four adults and a little luggage. However, in 1976 Ford eventually overtook British Leyland as Britain's best vendor of automobiles.

In January 1961, the Morris Mini Pick-up (and the Austin Se7ven Pick-up) arrived. This was interesting timing, since the Mini's immunity to the recession had

In January 1961, the Mini Pick-up arrived. NEWSPRESS

The Mini Pick-up featured a flat loading bay and drop-down tailgate. MAGIC CAR PICS

From 1961 to 1962 BMC also launched the Austin Super Se7en, which was essentially the same car as the existing A7, only with an improved interior and soundproofing. It was also given a two-tone paint job, incorporating a black or white roof, with a new grille that featured nine wavy horizontal bars and twelve straight vertical bars. It was therefore more expensive than both the base and range-topping models of the outgoing A7, at £592. The development of Mini models wouldn't stop there either: by 1963 there were eighteen different Mini models in four different marques, ranging from the basic saloons to the Riley Elf and Wolseley Hornet, as well as the estate cars and Mini vans.

Meanwhile on the other side of the world, BMC's Australian subsidiary had begun production of the Morris 850 at the Zetland plant in Sydney. In a report released by BMC for 1960 to 1961, the firm states that Mini production had risen by 62 per cent, despite a 10 per cent drop in the production of vehicles across the range. It was clear by this point that the Mini's presence was becoming a global necessity: everyone wanted to be driving a Mini. Back in the UK, BMC was realizing the demand for a more powerful Mini, one that could withstand the trials and tribulations on a race circuit. BMC introduced stronger steel wheels for the Mini, since many racing fanatics were shattering the standard rims under extreme high-speed cornering.

come to an end and its production had been hit hard, with only 2,000 cars rolling off the line each week. Nonetheless, this was still significantly higher than the production of other British cars at that time, and production picked up again a month later. The Pick-up utilized the same floorpan as the Austin Se7en and the Morris Mini Van, but instead featured a flat loading bay and a self-contained cabin – very much like a mini pick-up truck. There was even a drop-down tailgate fitted to the rear loading bay. Once again the Pick-up was run by the same 848cc engine, and priced at £360.

The Mini Pick-up utilized the same floorpan as the Mini Van. MAGIC CAR PICS

In the early 1960s, many folk were still slightly ignorant when it came to the purpose of the little Mini and what it stood for. But that didn't stop some more influential people noticing it, including John Cooper. He was aware of the Mini's core strengths, though this wasn't difficult since both of the Formula One drivers who raced for him, Jack Brabham and Bruce McLaren, were Mini owners and made a point of raving about them. John Cooper was more than aware of the little car's tuning potential too, having worked on Formula Junior cars with A-Series engines throughout his career. John Cooper did approach Sir Alec Issigonis on a number of occasions, trying to sell the idea of a performance model of his beloved Mini.

John Cooper with his son Mike. NEWSPRESS

LEFT: **John Cooper was aware of the Mini's core strengths and tuning potential.** MAGIC CAR PICS

BELOW: **John Cooper was instructed to build just 1,000 Coopers, which grew to 150,000.** MAGIC CAR PICS

Considering the fact that Issigonis had built this little car on the foundations that the Mini was an accessible vehicle for everyone, he wasn't too keen on the idea of building a more powerful variation.

But John Cooper wasn't going to give up that easily. His persistence saw him bypass Issigonis and go directly to George Harriman with a full proposal. Following that brief meeting, George Harriman told John Cooper to go away and build the performance Mini he was so keen to produce. John Cooper was instructed to build just 1,000 Mini Coopers, but this figure later turned into 150,000, proving Cooper's point. Oddly, the Cooper received a new internal

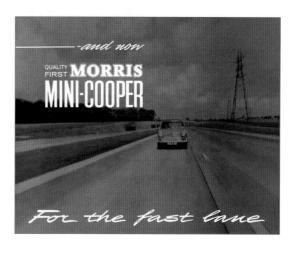

The Morris Mini Cooper S became a huge hit with motorists and celebrities. MAGIC CAR PICS

With the go-kart handling Cooper S the Mini entered the performance sector. MAGIC CAR PICS

project code, ADO50, while other Mini variants retained the ADO15 project code. This was quite odd, considering the fact that the Mini Cooper actually received fewer upgrades and amendments than models such as the commercial Mini Pick-up. The Mini Cooper was a huge success on the road too, becoming the performance car of the 1960s – quite an achievement for a little car that was never an official arrangement; John Cooper himself only earned a £2 royalty payment for the use of his name on each Cooper sold. But BMC's Cooper was a huge hit, and thanks to its success and countless celebrity endorsements, the rest of the Mini range saw a surge in sales.

The year 1961 was also the year that BMC announced two further Mini-themed variations: the Riley Elf and the Wolseley Hornet. These two cars were to be the more sophisticated Mini cars, with the Riley aimed to target the 'upmarket' segment. Writer and automotive journalist L.J.K. Setright said that the two cars were designed to 'appeal to those small-minded snobs who found the idea of a Mini intriguing but the name Austin or Morris offensive and the evidence austerity'.

Developed by BMC's senior stylist, Dick Burzi, the two cars featured an extended boot, vertical fins and revised detailing to the front end. Unlike the standard Mini styling elements, the Riley and Hornet were given a vertical grille, a wooden trim interior and extensive chrome detailing. To put it bluntly, neither of the two cars received great praise from the press. *Small Car* magazine, which later became *Car*, said:

The 'Super' and 'Cooper' twins were dubbed Britain's most challenging cars. MAGIC CAR PICS

The Riley Elf was designed to target the
'upmarket' segment. MAGIC CAR PICS

The Elf and Hornet were given a wooden trim
interior with chrome detailing. MAGIC CAR PICS

Unlike the Mini, the Elf and Hornet featured
a significantly larger boot space. MAGIC CAR PICS

BMC'S RESHUFFLE OF 1961

Heading towards the end of 1961 in early
November, BMC saw the first of many corporate
changes in the Mini's lifespan when Sir Leonard
Lord retired, to be replaced as chairman of
the firm by Sir George Harriman; Issigonis was
appointed BMC's technical director, and Charles
Griffin as the new chief engineer. By this point,
Issigonis had already divided the engineering staff
into three cells in order to streamline processes:
Cell A was headed by Jack Daniels and was
responsible for continuing the development of the
original Mini, Cell B was led by Chris Kingham and
worked on a new project known as ADO17, while
Cell C was directed by Charles Griffin and focused
on making progress on the forthcoming ADO16
project. Following the big reshuffle, the Austin
Se7en was renamed the Austin Mini, and BMC
claimed that Mini production had reached 3,800
cars per week.

*We guess it's no exaggeration to say that
the first Issigonis Wolseley Hornet was among
the ugliest, most uncomfortable and least
desirable cars ever offered to the Great British public. At any rate, the one we tested
in the winter of 1962 so disappointed us
we couldn't bring ourselves to write a word
about it.*

It is no surprise that Issigonis took a step back from
the two models, passing on full responsibility to

the development engineers and Dick Burzi. Funnily
enough, the Elf and Hornet models were supposedly
aimed at female drivers: they were said to resemble
miniature versions of a luxury saloon car, such as a
Jaguar, which appealed more to women. Not only
does that sound bizarre, but the overall design of the
new cars was already outdated, with their key design

LEFT: **The Elf and Hornet featured a revised front end and a vertical grille.**
MAGIC CAR PICS

BELOW: **In January 1963, Issigonis and Griffin demonstrated the Mini Moke prototype.**
MAGIC CAR PICS

elements slowly fading away as the world continued to progress deeper into the 1960s.

In August 1962, BMC finally revealed the project they had simmering on the back burner: Project ADO16 was announced as the Morris 1100. It was powered by a 1098cc A-Series engine, featured Pininfarina styling and Alex Moulton's Hydrolastic suspension. The Morris 1100 was a more refined and spacious example of the iconic small car, the Mini, and became Britain's best selling car for an entire decade. Although it only shared 10 per cent of its parts with the Mini, the two cars formed a partnership that dominated the British motor industry. In fact the Mini and its larger cousin, the Morris 1100, stood alongside the Jaguar E-Type and Ford's newly launched (and reasonably priced) Ford Cortina as the four cars that would define the 1960s. In November that year, *The Times* newspaper printed the following:

> In the last trading period the output on Minis reached 182,864 units, of which the home market absorbed 125,877. Exports are, however, increasingly steadily, and in the last three months of the financial year were averaging 1,308 a week.

One of the main events of 1963 was when the performance Mini Cooper was launched in Australia. But things were still busy back in the UK, as metal versions of the Countryman and Traveller estates were launched at a lower price than the outgoing woodframe models. Not only that, in January that year,

Issigonis and Charles Griffin demonstrated the twin-engined Mini Moke prototype outside the Longbridge factory. This event was mostly for the media, although a few familiar faces, such as comedy television star Norman Wisdom, made an appearance. After all, the Mini was a celebrity itself by this point. According to AR Online, George Harriman told *The Times*:

> This [the Moke] was originally conceived by Mr Issigonis and myself from the idea of an 0-8-0 locomotive, which has its wheels linked on either side. After producing some experimental versions, we found that the traction of the two Mini engines balanced each other, and that it was possible to run one in top gear and the other in bottom simultaneously.

It turned out to be a slow turnaround process though, the Moke reaching production form a year later, although the twin-engined version landed on a dead-end route. The Mini Moke was a very basic commercial vehicle, destined for the forces and light off-road usage. Priced as a mid-range vehicle at £405, it was produced until the early 1990s overseas, where it proved to be more popular than in Britain.

By this point it was also time for the Riley Elf and Wolseley Hornet sisters to be upgraded, and in January of 1963, Mk2 versions of the two cars were announced. These cars were powered by a single-carburettor 998cc engine, and were the first Mini models to be fitted with what would eventually become the reliable and tuneable, mainstream engine.

BMC waited until the Geneva Motor Show in March 1964 to announce the new cars: the Cooper

The Mini Moke was a very basic commercial vehicle destined for the forces.
NEWSPRESS

Mini PRODUCTION ROCKETS

Heading into the summer of 1963, the Mini Cooper 1071S was announced. This was followed by the news that, as the current technical director of BMC, Issigonis had been appointed to the main board of the firm. All the while, weekly production of the Mini was slowly creeping up the ladder, reaching more than 5,500. That year, the *Daily Express* is said to have reported: 'And it is a case of the Mini cars making a giant size impact on the market. For Mr Harriman also reveals that whereas in the previous year 60 per cent of his sales were cars under 1000cc, last year the production rose to 73 per cent of total output.' Meanwhile *The Guardian* wrote: 'The BMC Austin Mini and Morris Mini-Minor are four years old today

[30 August 1963]. A total of 662,337 Minis of all types has been produced, and 200,000 have been exported, 50 per cent to Europe and 25 per cent to Australia, were the Mini is the second bestselling car after the locally produced Holden.' In all truth, BMC had become entirely dependent upon production and sales volume to make its way in the world. The year 1963 was recorded as the firm's most successful year for the Mini: 134,346 Minis were sold in the UK in 1963, which dropped to a still notably impressive and very healthy 123,429 units the following year. Although the Mini remained strong until the very end of production in 1999, it never matched those sales figures again in its lifetime.

In 1963, the Mk2 Elf and Wolseley were the first Minis to run the legendary 998cc engine.

TOP: **In 1964, BMC announced the 970S and 1275S Cooper models.** MAGIC CAR PICS

ABOVE: **The Mini Cooper 1275S had 130mph (210km/h) at the pedal, and Hydrolastic suspension.** MAGIC CAR PICS

1964: A MAGIC YEAR FOR MINI

In February 1964, BMC was keen to announce its victorious figures behind Mini sales. The firm announced that it had built 1 million front-wheel-drive vehicles, and a grand total of 11,350 front-wheel-drive cars designed by Issigonis was rolling off the production line every week. Out of the 1,002,129 cars produced, 782,838 were Austin and Morris Minis, while 219,291 were Morris, MG and 1100s. Demand was forever increasing, presenting the perfect opportunity to launch two new Mini variants – it turns out there could never be too many Minis – although these two new cars were in a vastly different league to the Mini the world had become so familiar with.

970S and the 1275S. These cars wouldn't fall into the 'people's car' category since buyers would need to be generating a much higher income, especially in the case of the 1275S. Priced at £693, only 963 examples of the Austin and Morris Mini Cooper 970S (970cc) ever left the production line. It was vastly similar to the 1071cc Cooper S, aside from the engine, and was often referred to as the Mini-Cooper 1000. The Austin and Morris Mini Cooper 1275S (1275cc) featured a similar specification to the existing Cooper S models, only this one came with a 130mph (210km/h) centralized speedometer and Hydrolastic suspension. It remained in production until 1967, and was fitted with twin fuel tanks as standard from 1966. It was also the most expensive of the Cooper S line-up, at £778.

CHAPTER TWO

THE Mini GOLDEN YEARS

SUCCESS WITH THE STARS

By Christmas 1962, BMC had built more than half a million Minis, and just three years later that figure had doubled to a whopping 1,000,000. But the real success story came a year later, when continuing demand for the little car saw those numbers double once again to 2 million. Mini continued to hit manufacturing and sales milestones for the next sixteen years. Lord Stokes – the head of British Leyland Motor Corporation Ltd from 1968 to 1975 – celebrated the 3-millionth Mini to roll off the production line on 25 October 1972. In 1986, Noel Edmonds was on the scene to see the 5-millionth Mini roll off the line for Austin Rover.

In 1986, Noel Edmonds welcomed the 5-millionth Mini to the world.
MAGIC CAR PICS

Towards the end of 1964, BMC decided to let the media in on a little secret: it planned to fit all mainstream Minis with Alex Moulton's Hydrolastic suspension. However, this turned out to be a controversial decision. On a car that already struggled to make the firm any profit, engineers working on it found it difficult to see the potential in adding a notably costly feature to the range. And it turned out that the idea wasn't such a good one after all: while Hydrolastic suspension improved the car's ride, it compromised the handling, which was one of the Mini's key selling points, especially in Cooper and Cooper S form.

Furthermore, timing never played fair for BMC, and in September that year the Cowley factory began to suffer from unofficial strikes – and this wasn't good news for a car maker that depended solely on volume to make any money. This factory was primarily in charge of the Mini and ADO16 (the Morris 1100). To be precise, the factory witnessed 254 unofficial strikes, losing BMC at least 700,000 hours of production. So what did BMC do? It announced another product.

Codenamed ADO17, the Austin 1800 was powered by a B-Series engine, and was intended to sell at a higher price than the outgoing Morris 1100, therefore making the firm some extra cash to live on. But

it was a step too far, and not even Issigonis could make the 1800 a bestseller like his former creations. The Austin 1800 was far too large, heavy and expensive, especially to produce. In simple terms, ADO17 never witnessed the same success as the Mini and ADO16: it turned out that the Mini formula had hit a dead end. In fact, all the ADO17 achieved was greater recognition for Ford's Cortina, to Terry Beckett's delight.

The fact that the works Minis were disqualified from the Monte Carlo Rally in 1966 was actually one of BMC's smaller worries. The Mini of Timo Makinen and Paul Easter would have been crowned the winner for the third consecutive time if it hadn't been for a headlight infringement. But BMC went by the old

ABOVE: **The 998cc, 970cc and 1275cc S Hydrolastic models continued to thrill drivers.** MAGIC CAR PICS

RIGHT: **11,350 front-wheel-drive Issigonis cars were rolling off the line every week.** MAGIC CAR PICS

The Mini boasted the perfect package: a compact design with a pokey engine. MAGIC CAR PICS

AUTOMATIC TRANSMISSION MEETS TRANSVERSE ENGINE

In October 1965, BMC made history once again. The Mini and 1100 received new automatic gearboxes, further broadening the Mini's appeal. The transmission was a British-built system designed by the Automotive Products Group, and developed with BMC in a £3m joint investment. This was the first time that an automatic gearbox had been fixed to a transverse engine. The set-up was made possible with the addition of the engine sump, while a torque convertor replaced the clutch: it was the world's smallest automatic.

motto that 'There's no such thing as bad press', and continued without shame. In 1966, the boss of the newly acquired Pressed Steel Company, Joe Edwards, became managing director of BMC. His main task was to get the firm back on track and make financial figures look healthy again. To start things off, BMC and Sir William Lyons' Jaguar Group amalgamated to form British Motor Holdings (BMH). George Harriman was still chairman at this point, and had effectively taken over Jaguar. However, due to the re-election of the Labour government, new car trade slowed immensely. As a result, BMC – or more specifically, Joe Edwards – made 10,000 of its workers redundant, and altered a further 20,000 workers' shifts to part-time hours, as part of Edwards' rationalization plan.

This was a devastating time for the car maker, with an influx of protest strikes, even by delivery drivers – and if cars weren't being shifted from the plants, there was nowhere for them to go. BMC basically became overpowered by its own cars, meaning it had to shut down production completely and dealerships were left empty. The firm did recover (if you can say such a thing at such a time) by the end of the year, but the embarrassment it caused lingered until its final days. The public were growing tired of BMC's faults and it was rapidly losing market share. But in true BMC style, to make good of a bad situation the firm announced yet another reconstruction of the Mini's line-up: Mk3 versions of the Riley Elf and Wolseley Hornet. Ironically, the key differences were the eagerly anticipated wind-up windows, and the not-so-exciting internal door hinges.

The Mini did help BMC to redeem itself a little the following year, when Rauno Aaltonen and co-driver Henry Liddon claimed victory once again in a Cooper 1275 S – registration LBL 6D. Following its disqualification of 1966, the Mini had returned to claim back the trophy as a worthy winner. Celebrations, however, were short-lived, as by March it was reported that BMH had declared it had lost a whopping £7.5m since June the previous year. Although partnered with BMH, the British public and the government itself could already foresee the BMC's end, so much so that it actively encouraged a merger between BMH and Sir Donald Stokes' Leyland Motor Corporation. Since the Mini held a 15 per cent home market share in 1963, which slipped to 10 per cent in 1966 and down to 7 per cent in 1967, the little car urgently needed rescuing.

But it is argued that the decline wasn't due to the car itself being at fault, only BMC's inability to accommodate domestic demand in the UK; essentially, the firm was far too busy trying to impress markets overseas with set export figures. The newly appointed American Phil Paradise – former boss at Ford Italy – had become the managing director of BMC International Services, Europe and Switzerland. According to the press, he told reporters at the Frankfurt Motor Show: 'The Mini craze has brought much pleasure to a world that seems to enjoy expressing in a shorthand, diminutive way, and the Mini is a lot of automobile in a small package.'

As originally planned, the following year the facelifted Mk2 Austin and Morris Minis were launched. The Mk2 Minis were given a larger rear-view window and another restyled grille and rear light clusters. The Austin and Morris featured different grilles, but both cars offered the popular 998cc engine, which made its debut in the Riley Elf and Wolseley Hornet models. This didn't go smoothly though, since BMC's suppliers couldn't supply the new grille and rear light clusters in large quantity – or at least in the numbers required. Much like a flashback to the previous year, BMC ended up with 22,000 incomplete cars on its hands – it couldn't even produce enough 998cc engines. The supply chain issues lasted for approximately four months, fuelling the government's argument that the Leyland Motor Corporation was the only answer in restoring the British automotive industry.

Towards the end of 1967, Roy Hanes – the former chief stylist of Ford Britain who shaped the Mk2 Cortina – became BMC's director of styling. He also had a great deal of involvement with the development of the new Mk2 Mini. Sadly for the press, the Mk2 didn't get wind-up windows, and according to *Autocar* magazine 'some of the standards of fit and finish were disappointing'. But to BMC's delight, the leading motoring magazine did say the new car was 'a great improvement'.

THE END OF AN ERA

Production of the Mini ceased at the Cowley factory in January of 1968. From that moment on, Mini production was restricted to Longbridge. With the formation of British Leyland Motor Corporation (BLMC) many of the directors' responsibilities changed. Issigonis had practically lost all interest in the current line-up and wanted to dedicate his time to forward planning, in which he began work on designing a brand new Mini, which he codenamed the 9X. In 1968 BLMC officially came into existence, and although his time at the firm was short-lived, Joe Edwards resigned from BLMC due to heated tension between BMH and Leyland executives. Sir George Harriman remained chairman, while Sir Donald Stokes became the chief executive. But Harriman was already planning to stand down, and so Harry Webster – Triumph's technical director – was set to take over at the job at Longbridge, above Issigonis who was now busy working on the Mini's future at Cowley. He became the managing director of BLMC's Austin Morris division in September. Similarly, Roy Hanes was focused on producing the new Mk3 Mini and Mini Clubman. The same Harry Webster became chairman.

In May 1969, the final Issigonis design was revealed: the Austin Maxi. Based on the original Mini of 1959, the Maxi shared many similarities with the Morris and

ABOVE: **In 1968, the facelifted Mk2 Austin and Morris Minis were launched.** MAGIC CAR PICS

RIGHT: **The Mini Clubman became the icon of the 1970s, with a box-styled front end.** MAGIC CAR PICS

It's too good an idea for just one car

Ⓢ Mini

Austin Mini, but it consisted of a five-door layout and received a new overhead-cam engine, married to an in-sump five-speed manual gearbox. To cut a long story short, the Maxi wasn't a success. Riddled with engineering issues that impacted reliability, customers of 1969 were not willing to spend their money on a car plagued with issues as they had done previously with the Mini ten years before. Customers were getting tired of the Issigonis design philosophy, and this didn't impact well on Issigonis' reputation with the BLMC Corporation: sadly Issigonis was no longer an asset, but a liability. Although Issigonis was against such a creation, plans were calculated for an inline rear-wheel-drive 1275cc unit. This was mostly influenced by former Ford employee Roy Haynes. Following the formation of British Leyland, Haynes

wrote to finance director John Barber to push his plans of a rear-wheel-drive car, which was eventually launched as the Morris Marina. A month after the Austin Maxi was revealed, the 2-millionth Mini was completed – the Mini was the first British car to achieve such a result and, although he had little to no say in the further developments of the Mini range, the newly knighted Sir Alec Issigonis was there to see his baby roll off the production line. However, Austin Morris managing director George Turnbull was quick to praise Issigonis and his talents for producing innovative cars.

Upon promotion, Lord Stokes eventually returned from Europe with his team, which included Phil (Filmer) Paradise. He didn't see the need for re-badging the Mini, since it only caused confusion, and began phasing

RIGHT: **The final Issigonis design was revealed in 1969: the Austin Maxi.** MAGIC CAR PICS

BELOW: **Sir Alec Issigonis stands proudly with the 2,730,678th Mini.** NEWSPRESS

out different marque and model types, including the Riley Elf and Wolseley Hornet, which ceased production after 59,367 sales. In the autumn of 1969 production of the new Mk3 Mini and all-new Clubman officially began; the Mk2 models would be phased out by the end of the year. The Mini was finally given wind-up windows and internal hinges – improvements that publications such as *Autocar* had previously begged for – as standard across the range, and rebranding disappeared. Austin and Morris had been scrapped and the little car was now a Mini in its own right. The very last Mk2 Austin and Morris Minis left Longbridge in December 1969, but the last Cooper S was built on 23

February 1970. The refreshed Mk3 Mini was given a crash diet, losing Hydrolastic suspension for the old-fashioned rubber cones of 1959, and given chrome exterior detailing. It was produced in greater numbers: in 1971, 318,475 examples of the Mk3 Mini left Longbridge and overseas plants.

There was soon to be a new kid on the block, featuring a very distinctive nose. The Clubman was designed by Roy Haynes and his team of designers, and came in two forms. The Clubman estate featured the box-like nose and was powered by a 998cc engine; later, in 1975, it would be available with a 1098cc engine. Meanwhile, the sporty 1275 GT arrived to replace the existing 998cc Cooper. The Mini Clubman GT had Cooper S brake discs and a single 59bhp 1275cc engine, and while the Clubman estate rode on dry cone suspension throughout its production, the hot hatch used Hydrolastic until 1971. Priced at £834, the hatchback was well known for its 10in Rostyle wheels, manufactured by Rubery Owen – owners of the BRM Formula One team – for the

ABOVE: **The sporty 1275GT Clubman arrived in the mid-1970s, replacing the 998cc.** MAGIC CAR PICS

LEFT: **The Clubman estate featured the same box-like nose and a standard 998cc engine.** NEWSPRESS

first five years. These were changed to 12in wheels in 1974 to cover the front brake discs. The little hatchback also featured a close-ratio gearbox and an additional rev counter. As a whole, replacing the Riley and Hornet models with a Clubman was a good decision, and it proved much more successful.

By 1971, global Mini production had reached 278,950 units. After twenty-three years, the Morris Minor was withdrawn from production in April 1971; it was replaced by the rear-wheel-drive Morris

Marina mentioned a little earlier. Turning out to be a profitable company car, the Marina was actually a huge success, becoming Britain's second best-selling car in 1973. This wouldn't have pleased Sir Alec Issigonis, who had his heart set on the Project 9X, but the Marina took priority. The new Mk2 Cooper S arrived in July 1971, around the same time the Clubman GT hit the Australian market. Sir Alec retired from British Leyland in December of 1971, but he stayed on board as a consultant figure. Sir Alec was far too crucial and influential to the Mini badge for BL to let him go: the firm needed him. By the end of 1971, 258,427 Minis had left the production line at Longbridge, with a further 60,048 emerging from overseas, making a grand total of 318,475 Minis in one year.

Minis accounted for 30 per cent of BLMC's total vehicle production, and since the Marina had replaced the AD016 Morris 1100/1300, which ceased production at the Cowley plant, the Mini dominated the production lines at Longbridge. Nonetheless, the firm still wasn't comfortable financially. Despite that, BLMC managed to buy out Innocenti Autoveicoli of Milan in May 1972, which produced more than 700 Minis a week: this totalled at approximately 55,000 Minis every year. Geoffrey Robinson, BLMC's financial controller, became the new managing director of Innocenti. He focused on expanding Innocenti's exports, creating the Mini Cooper 1300, which was

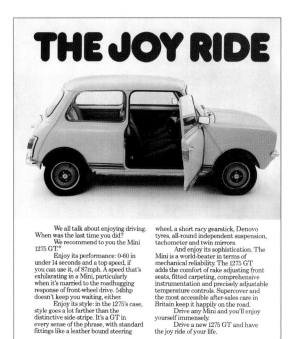

THE JOY RIDE

We all talk about enjoying driving. When was the last time you did?
We recommend to you the Mini 1275 GT.*
Enjoy its performance: 0-60 in under 14 seconds and a top speed, if you can use it, of 87mph. A speed that's exhilarating in a Mini, particularly when it's married to the roadhugging response of front-wheel drive. 54bhp doesn't keep you waiting, either.
Enjoy its style: in the 1275's case, style goes a lot farther than the distinctive side-stripe. It's a GT in every sense of the phrase, with standard fittings like a leather bound steering wheel, a short racy gearstick, Denovo tyres, all-round independent suspension, tachometer and twin mirrors.
And enjoy its sophistication. The Mini is a world-beater in terms of mechanical reliability. The 1275 GT adds the comfort of rake adjusting front seats, fitted carpeting, comprehensive instrumentation and precisely adjustable temperature controls. Supercover and the most accessible after-sales care in Britain keep it happily on the road.
Drive any Mini and you'll enjoy yourself immensely.
Drive a new 1275 GT and have the joy ride of your life.

HAPPINESS IS 🚗 SHAPED Mini

From Austin Morris with Supercover.
* Mini is a registered trade mark.

All performance figures courtesy of Motor Magazine.

REACHING THE THREE MILLION Mini MILESTONE

Back in the UK, BLMC persuaded the workers at Longbridge to accept measured day work in order to keep up with production overseas; by this point the Mini still retained its position as BLMC's best-seller across Europe. Lord Stokes was right when he said that in his opinion 'It is a dateless car that will go on for many years yet': truer words have never been spoken. At the London Motor Show in 1972 British Leyland celebrated the 3-millionth Mini, and Lord Stokes was confident that another 3 million Minis would be built, although it did take three decades – and he lived to see that day.

ABOVE: **The sporty Clubman hot hatch proved to be a hit, replacing the Elf and Hornet.** MAGIC CAR PICS

RIGHT: **By 1971, 258,472 Minis had left the production line at Longbridge.** NEWSPRESS

powered by a British-built 1275cc engine, featured disc brakes, and was overall a very stylish car of its time.

In 1973, ADO16 was replaced by the Austin Allegro. With its arrival all BLMC A-Series front-wheel-drive cars received a new rod change mechanism. The Mini was Britain's most popular export vehicle, being the firm's biggest selling car in Italy, Germany and Switzerland. Like Innocenti, BLMC also bought out its Spanish partner Authi in Pamplona, which meant that British Leyland now had full control of its European Mini manufacturing plants. In 1973 Authi began to build the Cooper 1300, which was very similar to the already launched Innocenti model. But since BLMC executives were starting to flee a sinking ship, it was difficult to see the point. This became clear in October, when the demand for small, economical cars rocketed due to another oil shortage caused by the Yom Kippur Arab-Israeli War: everyone wanted Minis again.

By 1974 the small-car market started to get serious. Ford was planning a new Super Mini, smaller than the Escort, to compete with the likes of Fiat's 127, the Renault 5 and, of course, the Mini. In June the last ADO16 was built, ending its long partnership with the Mini; the partnership was so successful that no other British car has ever been as popular worldwide. The then BLMC product planner John Bilton continued to find ways to reduce the Mini's significant costs,

finding that the 10in wheels were actually more costly than 12in. From the end of 1974, the 1275 GT was fitted with 12in wheels as standard – but it took another decade for the rest of the range to convert.

In February 1975 the Mini was officially dubbed Britain's best selling car, and the occasion was marked by a gathering of Austin Morris managing director Keith Hopkins and the one-and-only Sir Alec Issigonis. At this stage, the Mini and Maxi were the only Issigonis cars left in production. All Mini and most BL production came to a halt in April 1975, due to strikes at Dunlop. The British tyre market was responsible for the Mini's tyres and suspension cones, which wasn't good news at all. Thankfully, the matter was resolved by May, and production resumed. By this point Authi had built its last Spanish car – a Damask Red Mini – before BLMC ceased manufacturing cars in Spain. Soon after, in July, BL sold its Pamplona plant to SEAT for approximately £8.8m, which had produced 140,000 Minis. BL also announced it was putting its Italian subsidiary into liquidation, since it was already £10m in debt. Back in the UK, with British Leyland now split into four separate divisions, Mini production fell under Leyland Cars and the direction of Derek Whittaker. But by December it became public knowledge that Leyland Cars had experienced a £123m loss, and output had dropped by 17 per cent, as a result of the automotive recession.

By February 1975, the Mini was officially dubbed Britain's best-selling car.
MAGIC CAR PICS

CHAPTER THREE

REPLACING THE MINI

In 1976 Mini received an update, gaining interior fittings from the Austin Allegro and the Princess models, a modified suspension with softer springs and damper settings and new subframe mounts. By this point, the new facelifted Minis (Project code ADO20) were being assembled at Longbridge, while others were brought to the 'body in white' stage at Castle Browmwich. In true Mini style, ADO20 was only marginally profitable. However, in October the National Enterprise Board approved the programme to develop ADO88 at Seneffe in Belgium: a Super Mini to replace the Mini range. The new Super Mini was a necessary car, required to compete with Ford's all-new Fiesta, which was on its way, and to help cater for the UK market share, which had now dropped to 6.5 per cent. The Mini was surrounded by strikes, one of which took place at Rubery Owen and Darlaston, who supplied the Mini's subframe and wheels. But somehow Longbridge kept going, producing 160,000 Minis and welcoming the 4-millionth Mini to the road.

In 1977, production of the Mini Special (ADO88) began at Seneffe alongside the Austin Allegro. Its sole purpose was to replace the Clubman across Europe, since dealers found that European customers weren't too fond of the box-like hatch. Hitting dealerships on the continent from 1977, 73,753 examples were built until production ended in 1981. ADO88 was a round-nosed Mini powered by a 1098cc engine, in the hope of winning back the customers who appreciated Issigonis's design. By 1978, Michael Edwardes had become the new chairman of

Austin-Morris unveiled the 1100 Special to mark two successful decades.
MAGIC CAR PICS

Leyland Cars. He decided to produce two new versions of the old ADO20 project (the upgraded Mini) and a larger version of the ADO88, which would eventually become the Austin Metro. Since the Mini's design didn't seem to grow tiresome, its styling credentials played in its favour. Customers were already bored of the Fiesta and Renault 5, which all seemed to be too similar; the Mini was a completely different character. ADO88, however, was not like the desirable hatch: its larger LC8 size wasn't appealing, and it delayed production until 1980. Leyland Cars was renamed British Leyland Ltd that same year.

After two successful decades in production, the Mini reached its twentieth anniversary. Of course, Issigonis wouldn't have missed the moment for the world, and returned to the limelight to celebrate the occasion. Austin Morris unveiled the limited edition Mini 1100 Special to mark the milestone. Built at Longbridge, the 1100 was a classic round-nosed Mini and received the 1098cc engine. Finished in either Silver or Rose metallic paint, it was fitted with wide 10in Exacton alloys and was given extended wheel arches, although they were made of plastic. The Mini 850 was also rebranded the Mini City, but kept the small 848cc engine. The Mini City was available in two trims: the base level and the Super De

Luxe. The City Minis were a perfect example of BL reaching out to a more premium market. The standard 850 boasted check cloth upholstery with black bumpers and City decals, while the Super De Luxe had striped fabric seats, face-level ventilation and fitted carpets. Their prices were also a clear indication of the gradual change in the economy and the target market, with both 850 City cars priced at £2,482. Throughout the year, the Mini retained its 5 per cent market share, with the twentieth anniversary helping to push this figure up to more than 6 per cent by the end of the year.

This was indeed good news for BL, but resulted in a shortage of Minis at dealerships once again. Even though BL was importing 1,000 cars every month from Belgium, the 2,800 workers over in Belgium couldn't keep up with the UK's demand, therefore making this action redundant. Mini stock was now at a record low, even though production had still hit 165,502 by the end of the year, with UK sales totalling 82,938; the best of figures since 1975. Aside from the industry issues and financial flusters, the 1970s was the Mini's most successful decade, with 2,438,197 little cars hitting the road.

In 1980, BL was preparing for the launch of the Metro, while Austin Morris was making progress on

LEFT: **The 1100 was built at Longbridge and finished in Rose or Silver metallic paint.** MAGIC CAR PICS

BELOW: **The new Mini City was launched in 1980, powered by a 998cc A-Plus engine.** MAGIC CAR PICS

simplifying the entire Mini range. The Clubman Saloon and 1275 GT were phased out, but the Estate version was able to continue with a new name – Mini 1000 HL Estate – and a 998cc engine. Production of the Mini 850 City also came to an end, but it was replaced by the new Mini City, powered by a 998cc A-Plus engine – the same one destined to drive the new Metro. When the Metro was launched in October, it took the media by storm. In fact the Metro was dubbed the saviour of BL, although if it hadn't have been for the strong Mini sales, the Metro would never have made it to launch. The Mini suffered hard

ABOVE: **The all-new Mini City was launched the same year as the Metro.** MAGIC CAR PICS

RIGHT: **The Metro claimed an 8 per cent market share, weakening the Mini's power.** MAGIC CAR PICS

THE DEVELOPMENT OF THE A-SERIES ENGINE

In 1982 the last Mini Estate HL was built; it was then withdrawn from the range in September. Ahead of that, the Mini received higher gearing, mainly to keep the revs down, thus making it even more economical. This compromised the little car's acceleration performance. The A-Series engine was a remarkable creation, which explains why it was never re-engineered throughout its history – aside from developing overhead camshafts (ohc) for both the A- and B-Series engines back in the 1970s to maximize efficiency for exportation to America. The ohc B-Series unit evolved into an O-Series engine, while the ohc A-Series engine began to power the new ADO88 Mini and other BL cars. Eleven prototype ohc A-Series engines with aluminium cylinder heads were built in 1975 using Cooper S blocks in capacities of 970cc, 1097cc and 1275cc. Just think: fitted with the ohc 1275cc engine and twin HS6 SU carburettors, the sporty Clubman could reach an impressive 100mph (160km/h). However, adding an overhead camshaft to the standard A-Series engine pushed torque higher and often resulted in a number of technical issues. The standard A-Series engine has the ability to pull top gear and extremely low revs, but the ohc version – like in the 100mph Clubman – lacked this virtue, making everyday commuting a little too much of a handful. This is when BL launched the A-Plus programme.

when the Metro claimed an 8 per cent UK market share, and production at Longbridge plummeted to 1,150 cars per week. The Metro was now the hero, and the Mini was the public's future budget car.

The drama was far from over, however: in 1981 BL closed the Seneffe plant in Belgium, resulting in the loss of more than 2,500 jobs in both Belgium and back at Cowley in Oxford. As can be imagined, this caused an extremely bad atmosphere between Belgium and the UK. The workers at Seneffe had done a great deal for Mini across Europe, especially when UK plants were riddled with strikes, and understandably they felt betrayed. They demanded maximum redundancy payments, and as a bargaining measure more than 2,000 workers continued to work at the factory and blocked the departure of completed vehicles from the BL's European distribution centre, impounding 3,500 new cars: a crafty plan from the Belgium crew. To put the cherry on the icing, Rubery Owen closed its Darlastom factory, leaving BL looking for new suppliers of front subframes and wheels.

In 1982, Austin Morris was merged into the Austin Rover Group, under Harold Musgrove. This was the year that the Mini Mayfair was launched, an upmarket Mini for the wealthier classes. The Mayfair helped to push up Mini production from 940 to 1,050 per week, which meant that BL's plan to sell more higher-priced Minis was working. The following year, the very last Mini Van and Pick-up left the production line, after a successful output of 579,673 cars. The Mini's twenty-fifth anniversary was drawing closer, and was the perfect opportunity for Austin Rover to reveal the all-new Mini 25 anniversary edition. The Mini 25 was practically thrown together using old BL parts, which it no longer had use for. It reintroduced the 1275 GT's 8.4in front disc brakes and the significantly cheaper 12in wheels, which eventually became standard for all mainstream Minis.

THE MINI REVOLUTION

It is important to remember that the Mini's most successful year was twelve years into its life, in 1971. If the public didn't know it already, this was a strong indication that the Mini was no longer dependent on the success of its creators, and hugely admired and cherished by drivers of all ages. It wasn't until the Metro arrived in 1980 that the Mini ceased to become BL's bestselling car – but even then, the public were enthralled by the little car's achievement in completely altering the motoring industry – although it is slightly difficult to imagine the iconic small car being nicknamed 'the Metro's big brother'. It is fair to say that we very nearly lost the Mini altogether in 1986, as Austin Rover was so engrossed with the Maestro, Montego and Rover 200 that it planned to discontinue the Mini with the launch of the Austin AR6. Not only that, the Mini was a nightmare to

A-SERIES ENGINE SPECS

Performance ohc A-Series Specifications
970cc: ohc 59bhp @ 6,750rpm, 51lb ft @ 5,250rpm
1097cc: ohc 72bhp @ 6,500rpm, 64lb ft @ 5,000rpm
1275cc: ohc 84bhp @ 6,750rpm, 80lb ft @ 4,500rpm

Standard ohc A-Series Specifications
970cc: ohc 65bhp @ 6,500rpm, 55lb ft @ 3,500rpm
1071cc: ohc 70bhp @ 6,000rpm, 62lb ft @ 4,500rpm
1275cc: ohc 76bhp @ 5,800rpm, 80lb ft @ 3,000rpm
998cc: ohc 38bhp @ 5,250rpm, 52lb ft @ 2,700rpm
1098cc: ohc 45bhp @ 5,250rpm, 56lb ft @ 2,700rpm
1275cc: ohc 54bhp @ 5,250rpm, 67lb ft @ 2,500rpm

The 1275cc engine with twin carburettors meant the Clubman could reach 100mph (160km/h). MAGIC CAR PICS

manufacture, and by this point, out of date. But even the Metro couldn't hold the fort against Ford's Mk2 Fiesta, which eventually became Britain's best selling car in 1984.

Then in the 1980s a familiar face approached Austin Rover: John Cooper, who was responsible for the legendary Mini Cooper and Cooper S cars, wanted to bring back the legendary race-winner by fitting the Mini with the MG Metro engine. He even started creating and selling tuning kits for 998cc Minis, which were exported to Japan. By this point the Metro was ageing rapidly and was losing the love of its followers. In order to compete with Ford as well as General Motors and Vauxhall, Austin Rover had to pull something serious out of the bag. But while all this was going on, the sale of the 5-millionth Mini was slowly creeping up, and finally occurred on February 1986, with star guest Noel Edmonds. Mini adverts had even started appearing in the press again, including the 'Minis have feelings too' Christmas campaign in 1986. Apparently, research revealed that seven out of ten Mini buyers were women aged twenty to thirty-nine, a phenomenon that is said to have been triggered by that very same campaign, with women supposedly treating their little cars 'with affection', according to the *Daily Express* in an interview with Rover Group chairman Graham Day. Still a consultant for the firm, Sir Alec Issigonis wrote to Graham

Day to express his views on the Mini programme. These were not warmly welcomed, and resulted in his consultancy being terminated; and so the firm had

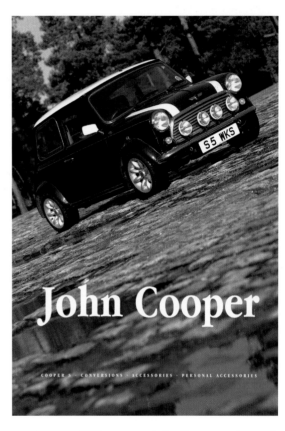

John Cooper

COOPER S · CONVERSIONS · ACCESSORIES · PERSONAL ACCESSORIES

THE MINI COOPER
IS BACK ON THE ROAD.
OCCASIONALLY.

It really took off back in the sixties, when it came first in over 25 major international rallies. Including, on three separate occasions, the Monte Carlo Rally. Today it comes with a 1.3 litre engine, a choice of Flame Red, British Racing Green or Black and a price of £6995. As anyone who drove the original will tell you, it's the only way to fly.

ABOVE: **John Cooper returned in the 1980s with new tuning ideas for the Mini.** MAGIC CAR PICS

LEFT: **In 1989, John Cooper returned to the board with a new performance upgrade kit.** MAGIC CAR PICS

The Mini was moulded into a variety of limited editions, including the Italian Job. MAGIC CAR PICS

now lost the Mini's three greatest warriors – Downton, John Cooper and Issigonis himself. The Mini was also moulded into a variety of limited editions in the 1980s, including the Mary Quant 'Designer' and the 'Italian Job' models.

To mark the end of the 1980s, John Cooper returned to the board in 1989, with his already established performance upgrade kit available as an optional extra on all 998cc Minis. By this point, Austin Rover had become Rover Cars, making the Mini an official Rover. Sadly, Issigonis didn't live to see the thirtieth anniversary of his baby, but this occasion was marked with a forty-second TV advert, featuring actress and model Twiggy, taking viewers right back to the swinging 1960s and on a bumpy ride through its historic journey. The tagline for the advert was simple:

'You never forget your first Mini.' The fact that the Mini was already a classic, but still continued in production, highlighted its importance. The Mini had performed its duty as a small budget car that had gone on to reach the top. To celebrate this success, John Cooper launched the John Cooper LE (Limited Edition), of which just 300 were made for the UK only.

It was in July 1990 that the Mini Cooper LE was sent into production. The Rover Special Products (RSP) Cooper was extremely last minute. Just as John Cooper had previously suggested to Graham Day, the new Cooper cars were powered by a (catalysed) 1275cc MG Metro engine. Since demand was sky high, Rover launched a mainstream version of the Cooper two months later. The resurrection of the Cooper boosted Rover sales significantly, outselling the

Under the instruction of Rover, John Cooper launched the John Cooper LE. NEWSPRESS

The return of John Cooper secured the Mini's survival in the twenty-first century.
MAGIC CAR PICS

In the 1990s, the Mini Cooper became every young petrol-head's dream.
NEWSPRESS

John Cooper's Mini featured a bold interior with an intensely modern dashboard.
NEWSPRESS

standard Mini; the return of John Cooper is what secured Mini's survival into the twenty-first century, eventually attracting BMW. Following on, the final changes the Mini witnessed were to its engine. By 1992, the Mini was no longer powered by the 998cc engine: instead, the base model – now called the Sprite – was powered by a standard 1275cc engine, which sat below the higher-spec Mini Mayfair.

After forty-one years in production, the very last Mini was driven off the production line to the Quincy Jones' soundtrack of *The Italian Job* film in the year 2000. Hundreds gathered at Longbridge to watch the emotional yet proud moment. Many of the surviving members of Issigonis's team were also in attendance, and the car was driven by production line supervisor Geoff Powell, with star singer Lulu by his side. The very last of 5,378,776 Minis is now kept at the Heritage Motor Centre in Gaydon, alongside many other members of the Mini family.

1990 SALES FIGURES

Longbridge produced 46,045 Minis, out of which:
10,067 Minis were sold in the UK
12,087 Minis were exported to Japan
8,977 Minis were exported to France
4,790 Minis were exported to Germany
2,680 Minis were exported to Italy

By 1992, the Mini base model with the 1275cc engine was now called the 'Sprite'. MAGIC CAR PICS

After forty-one years, the final Mini was driven off the production line in the year 2000. MAGIC CAR PICS

Mini AND MINI IN THE TWENTY-FIRST CENTURY

More than fifty years on, the classic Mini remains at the heart of every motoring enthusiast's car collection. The Mini is a hobby, a lifestyle, and in many cases, a member of the family. Ask any Mini driver and it is highly likely that the chances are that they've named their car. In contrast, BMW's take on an iconic British family car has also found its way into the hearts of many motorists worldwide, alongside its older and significantly smaller predecessor. The Mini of 1959 led the way to fashion in motoring, and the MINI of 2000 led the way to infinite customization – or at least that is how the story is usually told. It is quite possible that no other machine on four wheels has even been so admired and so adored by drivers past and present.

But while the Mini and MINI share the same ethos, they are vastly different, for all the right reasons. The MINI of today is vastly different to that of the past, and that is possibly one of its greatest achievements. BMW have managed to design and build a car that closely resembles its predecessor, but with the modern characteristics to compete in today's automotive market.

Essentially, BMW have encouraged a new generation of car enthusiasts by building on the foundations of the original car and transforming it into a modern masterpiece. While it maintains strong links with the revolutionary classic, it is slightly larger, it is safer, it is equipped with all the latest modern-day gadgets and gizmos, and it has a brand new style. But unlike the majority of other vehicles on the road, the Mini and the MINI will always be desired and cherished

More than fifty years on, the classic Mini still has the power to steal our hearts away.

NEWSPRESS

by thousands of motorists around the world – their most important similarity.

Since its launch in 1959, the Mini was remoulded into a number of model variants, and this tradition has been closely followed by BMW: the sportier Mini Cooper, the Mini Van, the Countryman, the Traveller, the Moke and the Pick-up. Each model to follow the new MINI hatchback has been similar to the retro range of the 1960s and 1970s, although the model names have been somewhat varied. The Clubman, for example, was a desirable flat-nosed hot hatch in its original form, but is now a small yet practical family estate. Similarly, the Countryman has evolved from a classic estate into a modern-day crossover.

Paying homage to its past roots, the MINI hatchback, Clubman, Convertible, Coupé and Roadster variants of the German-owned brand are assembled at Plant Oxford in Cowley; the more recent Countryman and Paceman models are pieced together by Magna Steyr in Austria.

BMW have created a modern-day masterpiece, which pays homage to its predecessor.
NEWSPRESS

PART II
*MINI: REPLACING
A LEGEND*

CHAPTER FOUR

THE ARRIVAL OF BMW

From the start, replacing the Mini was never going to be an easy task, and it is still regarded as one of the toughest challenges to face the automotive industry. After all, the Mini single-handedly reshaped the face of the motoring industry. In 1990, in *Autocar* magazine, a panel of 100 automotive experts voted the Mini the UK's most significant car of the century, ahead of the VW Beetle, the Ford Model T and the Citroën DS.

Like most classic cars, the original Mini – the very first to leave the production line – was deemed irreplaceable: a car that should be left to grow old gracefully and never be altered. But that wasn't enough to stop BMC and its ancestors from trying. A number of contenders tried to follow in the footsteps of the Mini and match its criteria, yet failed, mostly due to costs. Even Issigonis himself couldn't produce another car in its league. The new MINI saw two

manufacturers go head-to-head in a battle for the final say, yet they unwillingly worked together to produce the final masterpiece; so it turns out that the development of the new MINI was one of the most controversial in history.

The Issigonis 9X of 1968 was cancelled by BLMC due to costs, followed by the Barrel Mini that very same year. In 1973 the ADO74 was also cancelled by BLMC due to costs, and between 1974 and 1975 it was considered that it would be too costly to build the Innocenti Mini at Longbridge. In 1977 the ADO88 became the Metro. The 9X would have been the car to advance the Mini concept, which Issigonis himself had believed would be a certainty in 1970 in order to keep the Mini alive. But the Mini, of course, was no ordinary car, and the death of its never-to-become predecessor allowed the original to live on, and on, and on, just as it still does today.

Replacing the Mini was one of the most controversial challenges to face the industry.
NEWSPRESS

The Innocenti Mini was deemed too costly to build at Longbridge.
MAGIC CAR PICS

Rover began to realize the Mini couldn't continue in production in its original form.

Rover began serious work on the development project in the 1990s, when the A-Series engine was unlikely to pass emissions regulations and drive-by noise ratings. The fact that the A-Series engine had already been replaced by the K-Series in the rest of the range meant that the reasons to continue producing it had begun to wear thin, and it had become uneconomical. With safety becoming increasingly important and the requirement for airbags and the need to pass the EuroNCAP test just around the corner, the realization that the little Mini would be unable to accommodate such devices and therefore past the test was becoming a firm reality.

Not only that, the Mini itself was labour intensive, being mostly built by hand with a touch of good old-fashioned sweat and elbow grease. This made the Mini a car that workers at Longbridge found challenging to produce, and it would not continue. For this very reason the Metro would also need replacing. The UK's automotive industry was about to begin work on one of the most controversial projects in all history. Rover's attempt at rebuilding the Mini, which began in the year 1993, was soon strengthened by the arrival of BMW the following year. The outcome caused controversy amongst many enthusiasts, but went on to steal the hearts of thousands of buyers across the world.

HYDRAGAS AND HYDROLASTIC SUSPENSION

Hydragas suspension was pioneered by British Leyland. When the Mini was launched in 1959, the British Motor Corporation (BMC) – British Leyland's predecessor – was at the forefront of innovative automotive engineering. In the late 1950s, a system called Hydrolastic was founded by Dr Alex Moulton, designed to replace conventional suspension units with fluid-filled displacers containing a rubber spring, and interconnected with fluid-filled pipes to make them sit level. The original Mini was supposed to receive Hydrolastic suspension for its launch in 1959, but co-developers and Dunlop Tyres couldn't produce small enough displacers in time. But not all was lost, and when the fast-selling 1100 was launched in 1962, the British nation soon became familiar with the 'Moulton bounce'. In the 1960s, BMC refined the Hydrolastic system by fitting it to the Austin 1800, the Austin 3-litre, the Austin Mini and the Austin Maxi.

Then in 1970, the Hydrolastic system was replaced by technology that would forever be remembered for its association with the Austin Allegro. Hydragas cars had displacers that were partially filled with nitrogen, separated by a rubber membrane, thus providing an all-new form of suspension. As in the earlier cars, Hydragas suspension was interconnected: when a wheel hit a bump, the aim was for the suspension to compress, pushing fluid down the interconnecting pipe to the unit at the rear. This didn't work particularly well on the early Allegros because the damping wasn't strong enough, and engineers at Longbridge worked to resolve the issue by improving the system – not that Allegro customers would ever trust the suspension again. But all was not lost, because when Austin's beloved Princess came along, it featured a refined Hydragas system, which resulted in a more than satisfactory ride and handling.

Sadly, by the time the Princess was launched in 1975, British Leyland was staring bankruptcy directly in the eyes. When Spen King – designer of the Rover SD1 and the Range Rover – was instructed to produce an efficient range of future BL cars, he decided that Hydragas was too complex and far too costly; as a result, the new Allegro and Maxi replacement lost Hydragas altogether and was given a carbon copy of the Volkswagen Golf's MacPherson strut-and-beam axle set-up: this was the Maestro. But it wasn't the end for Moulton's creation – far from it, in fact. BL was still working on a new 'super mini', and due to company funds draining away like water, built a little car by throwing together Mini and Allegro parts. This was christened the Metro.

2 Million British Leyland Motorists Ride Safely on Moulton Hydrolastic® Suspension

MINI 1275 GT

Intercoupled front-to-rear HYDROLASTIC springing provides a smooth controlled ride, steadied at high speeds and softened at low speeds.
With damping inbuilt, the springing characteristics remain as designed throughout the service life of the car, without maintenance.
The HYDROLASTIC spring units are exclusively manufactured for the Corporation by:

THE DUNLOP COMPANY LIMITED
ENGINEERING GROUP (SUSPENSIONS DIVISION)
COVENTRY

Hydrolastic suspension was founded by Dr Alex Moulton in the late 1950s.
MAGIC CAR PICS

In 1993, the first design elements of the new Mini were shown at Canley design studios, but while Rover was racking its brains for ideas of how to go about replacing the Metro, it made perfect sense that this new car would replace both. Product design director Gordon Sked at Rover Group worked with his design team to produce a variety of ideas for the new Mini, no matter how eccentric or adventurous they turned out to be. The Mini was neither subtle nor restrained, and this was to be highlighted through its appearance. This resulted in the designers, including David Saddington and David Woodhouse, drawing up an entire range of potential Mini models. A number of concepts was considered, including the three-seater city car with McLaren styling and a prototype nicknamed the 'Minki' – featuring the K-Series engine and Hydragas suspension – but Rover soon found itself being sold to the mighty manufacturer BMW, and had no idea how the Bavarian Motor Works company would approach the Mini project.

To begin with, the Rover designers were relieved to find that the head of BMW, Bernd Pischetsrieder, was more than happy for them to carry on with their original design briefs to shape the new Mini. Being the great-nephew of Issigonis himself, Pischetsrieder was very well aware of the Mini's great sentimental value to the British population, and felt that it was important for the Rover team to work independently from the BMW headquarters in Munich, Germany. After all, who was better placed to design and build the new British icon, other than the British themselves? After providing the funding to continue the Mini rebuild alongside a real codename – R59 – Pischetsrieder even made it his responsibility to build a trustworthy project team, recruiting the remaining masterminds of the original ADO15 project. These included John Cooper, Jack Daniels and Alex Moulton.

Inevitably, in 1994 the German car maker was keen to get more involved with the new Mini replacement project. Stylists in Munich were already working on new proposals for a modern-day Mini, and it turned out that their visions of the new car differed greatly from those of Rover. While David Saddington, who had been promoted to design director of MG and Mini, wanted to produce another car that closely resembled its predecessor, the rest of the Rover and BMW clan had fresh ideas in mind. It was clear by this point that 'the car' was becoming more than just a car: it was now a fashion icon that needed to be equipped with higher standards of safety equipment and in-car gadgets, to produce low economy figures, and – even for a Mini – to boast more cabin space – where imagination meets practicality. Of course, combining each of those key elements was never going to be an easy target.

BMW focused on designing a new Cooper, wondering what the car would have looked like if it had gone on to become a continuous design project like the beloved Porsche 911. NEWSPRESS

At the time, Chris Bangle – labelled as one of the most controversial designers in automotive history – was busy conjuring up a design recipe that would both please and disgust. He was working on a new 'Mini Cooper', with a goal to produce a brand new car that wouldn't be overshadowed by the classic. In his eyes, the new Mini was to be an all-new icon car in its own right. By this stage, BMW was focusing on producing a new Cooper, rather than just a Mini, desperately trying to imagine what the car would have looked like in the mid-1990s had it gone on to become a continuous development project in the same way as the beloved Porsche 911. Enter BMW's product development chief Wolfgang Reitzle – the man who battled with Joachim Milberg to secure the BMW chairman's seat in 1999, and lost – and enter the problem: Rover was adamant on building an eco-friendly runaround, while BMW was determined to produce a small sports car – what we now call the 'hot hatch'.

In 1995, Rover revealed their idea for the new Mini, which turned out to be exactly what we all predicted: a four-seater cube, following in the path of a K-Series engine, subframes, and of course Hydragas suspension. Meanwhile, BMW was working on another alternative, featuring a rear Z-axle and MacPherson struts at the front. There was only one solution: on 15 October 1995, BMW and Rover designers gathered at the Heritage Motor Centre in Gaydon to present their full-scale prototypes – you can only image the tension between the two brands. While Rover's three model proposals were documented – the Evolution, Revolution and Spiritual – BMW refused to record exactly what, or how many cars they presented. The Spiritual proposals, called Mini and Midi, were said to have been shown in long-wheelbase form, proving that the design could also work in a larger package. Meanwhile, BMW's models represented sporting cars, none of which paid homage to Issigonis' original, aside from details of retro exterior styling. The mastermind behind one of these cars was American automotive designer Frank Stephenson.

Pischetsrieder, Reitzle and the Rover board members would have the final say as to which designs were to be taken forwards, and both Stephenson's and Saddington's models caught their attention. They decided these models captured the conventional small car qualities and combined them with

In 1995, Rover and BMW gathered at the Heritage Motor Centre, Gaydon, to reveal their designs. Rover's turned out to be what we predicted: a four-seater cube with Hydragas suspension. MAGIC CAR PICS

the retro sporting appeal that the two manufacturers were looking for. Pischetsrieder was impressed by Rover's concepts, but believed they were too far ahead of their time – he was looking for a simple design that wouldn't age too quickly, but would also fit in with the current-day motoring crowd, enabling the company to get the car into production as quickly as possible. Rightly so, he was looking for a car that would reflect the spirit of a Mini for the twenty-first century. The Spiritual concept was therefore pushed aside, regardless of Rover's efforts to push it forwards. However, its spacious qualities were recognized as a crucial element for the new car. In the end, Rover's head of design Geoff Upex made the final decision. At the time, it was probably seen as a shocking choice, but today it was arguably predictable. Upex appointed Saddington to be the car's design chief, leaving the Brits in charge of the overall Mini package, and American designer Stephenson responsible for its styling.

CHAPTER FIVE

BMW'S TAKE ON
A BRITISH ICON

Developing the new Mini was never going to be a smooth procedure. Saddington and Stephenson would continue to argue over designs, while they learned that packaging the new Mini was tougher than expected. Project management and engineering was handled by BMW in Munich, while Stephenson was working as a BMW employee within Rover back in Gaydon: this meant that little progress was made. Therefore in May 1996 the entire project was handed back to Rover, renamed Project R50, and managed by new project director Chris Lee. This didn't bode well with the Munich team, so BMW's development chief Burkhard Goeschel was sent to oversee the handover, which then became rushed. The Rover team had inherited a BMW platform – which had been decided upon in 1995 – but no one knew which engine and gearbox it would run, and even worse, no one had informed Moulton or BTR Development

that their work on the new Mini was no longer required, leaving the 'Minki II' prototype, which had met all the requirements asked of it by BMW, redundant by September 1996.

By the end of 1996 it became apparent to Rover that the Mini's new chassis decisions were firmly in BMW's hands. To ensure there were no slip-ups, BMW organized a new, second team to be set up in Munich. This team would act as a guardian for Rover, someone the team back in Britain could call upon during the development of the new car. As you can imagine, this process was not particularly helpful or welcomed. The manager of the R50 project, Chris Lee, became what you might refer to as the 'piggy in the middle', trying to make sense of and find peace between the two sides.

If that wasn't enough, Rover itself was also having issues with Wolfgang Reitzle, who had frozen the

In May 1996, the project was codenamed R50 and directed by Chris Lee. MAGIC CAR PICS

R50's styling when the engine and gearbox had yet to be confirmed. On Rover's behalf, Saddington had already made his concerns clear by highlighting the fact that by using the existing low bonnet line, the K-Series engine would be a worryingly tight fit, and therefore pressed the point that it should be raised. But meanwhile, on the other side of the fence, BMW blamed the K-Series engine for 'not having a space-efficient package'. According to the press, Wolfgang Reitzle took upon himself to tell Saddington that he would fix the problem, without actually stating how and when he would do it.

It is possible to imagine the frustration of the engineers working on Project R50, since the car they were now preparing was no longer the car they felt was destined to replace the Mini – BMW had well and truly taken over the project, and there was no turning back. If losing all say over the new vehicle's design elements wasn't enough for the engineers back at Gaydon, in Warwickshire, Wolfgang Reitzle stayed good to his word and eliminated another question hovering over the project, when he later announced that BMW would co-develop a brand new engine for a brand new Mini with Chrysler, which was to be built in Brazil. That's right: the K-Series engine – the replacement for the original A-Series unit – was no longer a contender for the new car.

It is important to remember that, although the majority of decisions surrounding the MINI project were made by BMW, it was in fact the British engineers from Rover who carried out most of the work, specifying and designing components at Rover's engineering centre at Gaydon. The only requirements set by BMW were the MacPherson strut front and rear Z-axle formation. Even the MINI's engine and gearbox were engineered at both Longbridge and Gaydon, and at this point there were possibly more than 400 British engineers working on the new MINI. Although BMW was set upon having a Getrag gearbox for the new car, the UK team mated the engine to a Midland R56 transmission instead, mainly because it was £100 per car cheaper and it was more compact. The R56 gearbox was far from being a new creation, since it was already being manufactured at the Longbridge site and was making an appearance in front-wheel-drive Rover cars. It was an easy argument to win, but by keeping evidence of

back-to-back tests as well as performance and service evaluations, the Brits eventually won the battle with Rover's R56.

Once the engineers knew what would be at the heart of the new MINI, they could finally make focus on the final build, producing what would become the 'production release' or 'concept' cars. The Rover team began development with simulators, of which there were two versions: Rover 200s with a mock Mini chassis, and 200s with the new MINI's Pentagon engine. All the while the engineers had to remember the main aim of the game: to produce the best handling front-wheel-drive car in the world. It turns out that the rear Z-axle set-up was a hit. Any talk of wishbones was frowned upon, however, since BMW insisted that the MINI was a BMW and therefore had to feature struts. Due to having a compact front end, it was inevitably difficult to set up the suspension and minimize torque steer.

To Rover's horror, BMW was adamant that the new car would have no resemblance to the original – or at least, it wouldn't be based on the same foundations. BMW's MINI would be a new car in its own right, marking the beginning of a new era and one that had a spot in the future. But that didn't stop the original Mini running alongside the new one – and in fact, in most cases, the little Mini continued to outshine its successor, championing in motor racing, thrilling crowds at shows and altogether stealing the limelight. BMW were going to have to pull something out of the bag to make it work.

The MINI was to be a small, premium hatchback, meaning its price tag was inevitably going to rise, but not quite reaching the figures of BMW cars such as the 3 Series. However, the fact that the new car was destined to target BMW rather than Rover buyers meant that the extra cash needed to own one of these little cars wouldn't be too much of an issue. BMW already boasted a global dealer network of more than 4,000, and since the brand was (and still is) renowned for its high quality cars, surely they'd have no problem selling this new one under the BMW umbrella alongside Land Rover, MG and Rover? Well, you'd think not. But for many Mini enthusiasts, the new car was an insult. It was too big and too German. How could it possibly replace the British pocket-rocket?

THE CONCEPT CARS

The ACV30

It was the ACV30 concept of 1997 that gave us the first real glimpse of BMW's direction for the little car. They actually announced this car – a retro-styled coupé – at the Monte Carlo Rally. It was built on an MGF chassis, and reflected similarities of the Dream-works proposal of the new car at Gaydon in 1995. While it is clear to see that this concept does carry some familiar BMW MINI DNA, its appearance did little more than prove to the world that Rover and BMW were working seriously on a replacement for the Mini, and that it would be vastly different to the car they knew all too well. Nevertheless, it did help to soften some peoples' views on the arrival of the new car, and at last they weren't preparing for the unknown, but were contemplating the sight of what could be the new car. Features such as the centrally mounted speedometer were present in the ACV30

BELOW: **AVC30 was built on an MGF chassis and resembled BMW-styling characteristics.** MAGIC CAR PICS

LEFT: **The ACV30 MINI Anniversary Concept Vehicle, which celebrated twenty years of the hat-trick of Mini wins at the Monte Carlo Rally, pictured here with Rauno Aaltonen's Monte-winning Mini Cooper LBL 6D.** NEWSPRESS

BELOW: **The AVC30 1997 gave us a glimpse of what the BMW MINI would look like.** MAGIC CAR PICS

concept, and filtered down into the MINI we know today. In fact, the centralized speedometer is one of the MINI's most symbolic assets, along with the rest of the interior, which was inspired by the ACV30 and tweaked by Britons Wynn Thomas and Tony Hunter.

The Rover Spiritual

Next up was the Rover Spiritual, which made an appearance at the 1997 Geneva Motor Show. Designed by Oliver Le Grice, the Spiritual was what we'd call a rear-engined city car today. Issigonis would not have been impressed with the engine set-up, since he believed that rear-engined, rear-wheel-drive cars were unsafe and should be banned by the law. The Spiritual was just 10ft (3m) long, too, just like the original Mini. It was also designed with a short and long wheelbase, with the longer version christened the Midi. Like the ACV30, the Spiritual had been taken to Gaydon in 1995 to decide which car would eventually go into production. It was said to be at least a decade ahead of its time, earning praise from BMW Group boss Bernd Pischetsrieder, though it didn't earn too much praise from the public.

Sadly, neither the ACV30 nor the Rover Spiritual ever made it past the concept stage, and they remain another figment in the 'Mini makeover' history books. By this point both the public and the media were on tenterhooks, waiting for the official unveiling of THE new mock-up MINI: this would be revealed at the Frankfurt Motor Show just a few months later.

THE FIRST RUNNING CONCEPT OF THE MINI

When the first running concept of the MINI was revealed at the Frankfurt Motor Show, its interior resembled that of the ACV30, and we would come to learn that it was identical to the car that would be launched two years later in production form. However, at this point the MINI was nowhere near ready for production – this mock-up concept was based on a modest Fiat Punto. But there was some good news, with the overall atmosphere surrounding the MINI becoming much more positive, even between BMW and Rover. But that's not to say that it stayed that way, since Rover and BMW were arguably as compatible as chalk and cheese. The final stages of

the MINI development progressed as you'd expect: more prototypes were designed and built, road-testing commenced, and it also took quite a thrashing around the Nürburgring in Germany to tweak and finalize the car's set-up. BMW has been fine-tuning chassis at the world's most iconic yet treacherous racing circuit for generations. So while BMW took over testing, Rover was in charge of production, with the new MINI still destined to be built at the factory in Longbridge. But the trials and tribulations continued in the final build-up.

To Rover's surprise, BMW's development chief Burckhard Goeschel fired the MINI project director Chris Lee, which wasn't exactly the most appropriate timing, and was arguably unjust treatment for a man who had dedicated so much time and effort into getting the final MINI ready for production. Nevertheless, the show must go on, and the MINI story continued with one more hurdle to jump. The two big names at BMW – CEO Pischetsrieder and product development chief Reitzle – resigned from the brand and therefore the project. Rover's ally, at the head of the brand, had disappeared, leaving the British team helpless to defend its role in the final build stages. Instead, BMW placed project R50's original brand director Heinrich Petra back in the driving seat, and stripped Rover of all its responsibilities. Once again, this little car in the making was causing quite a stir, with two manufacturers battling for the limelight. Would the new MINI ever be completed?

In 1999, the final development of Project R50 was taken under the wings of BMW. But the majority of the engineers who had worked endless hours for more than three years to create the new car stood their ground and remained in Britain with Rover. Times were bleak, and the head of the venture capital group Alchemy Partners Jon Moulton agreed to buy loss-making Rover cars from BMW, ending Rover's days as a mass-market car maker and posing a threat to at least half of the 10,000 people working at Longbridge. Jon Moulton eventually backed down, leaving the way for the Phoenix consortium to buy the firm. According to the BBC, Jon Moulton said through gritted teeth that the government's role in backing Phoenix helped BMW save £1bn: 'The government made it easy for BMW to get out of Rover at a relatively low cost.'

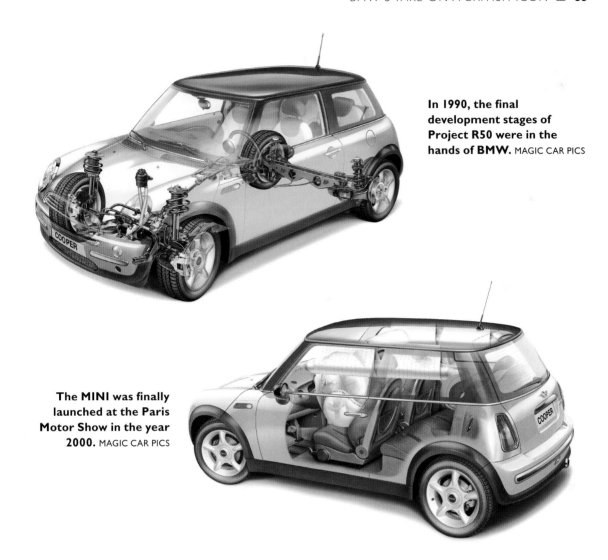

In 1990, the final development stages of Project R50 were in the hands of BMW. MAGIC CAR PICS

The MINI was finally launched at the Paris Motor Show in the year 2000. MAGIC CAR PICS

The BBC also released a quote from a spokesman for former government minister Stephen Byers, assuring that the new owners of Rover were focused on making the firm a mass-market manufacturer once again: 'Our position at the time was to safeguard jobs. It was a commercial decision by BMW.' At the beginning of the year 2000, Longbridge's involvement with the new MINI came to an end, and BMW was keen for all digital files and documents surrounding Project R50 to be downloaded on to German hard drives – the brand was aiming for a January 2001 sale target, and the partnership with Rover was over.

The MINI was at the heart of the one of the greatest conflicts in the automotive industry, and was dragged into BMW's MG Rover sell-off in the year 2000. John Towers, one of the four business-men who founded the Phoenix Consortium, is said to have pleaded with BMW to allow the car to re-main under British control, with production begin-ning at Longbridge as originally planned. It was no surprise that BMW broke this promise. The brand had already seen what the power of the Mini mark could do, especially in Britain, and wanted to keep the success story all to itself. BMW had the MINI's production facility moved to Cowley, now known as BMW Oxford or Oxford MINI, which saw the pro-duction of Rover 75 vehicles moved to Longbridge. Thankfully, that was the end of the conflict.

Four years after the prototype had been revealed, the first MINI rolled off the production line at Plant Oxford in 2001.
NEWSPRESS

LAUNCHING THE MINI

The MINI was finally launched at the Paris Motor Show in the year 2000, with BMW insisting that the brand name would be capitalized. The MINI was to be a game changer, and the media knew that. The entire management team made an appearance at the big unveiling, with BMW's development chief Burkhard Goeschel and chief designer Frank Stephenson on hand to answer questions surrounding the MINI as a product when the cover was finally whipped from the car for the crowds to see. At the show, Stephenson said: 'The MINI Cooper is not a retro-design car, but an evolution of the original. It has the genes and many of the characteristics of its predecessor, but is larger, more powerful, more muscular and more exciting than its predecessor.'

Since it had been four years since the new car had been revealed in prototype form, buyers were keen to place their orders and the journalists were keen to get in it, which inevitably wouldn't take long. The first MINI to hit the UK market rolled off the production line in July 2001. BMW remained original with their marketing ideas, with a 'MINI adventure' campaign, well packaged to target the young drivers whose parents understood the importance and heart-warming memories of the classic, which they undoubtedly once owned themselves and held dear

to their hearts – although when it came down to it, many Mini enthusiasts were bitter towards the new car, which was to be expected. After all, it wasn't technically a British-owned car, and resembled very little of Issigonis's Mini they had come to adore. But the new car was, and still is, a Brit at heart, mostly because of the hundreds of British engineers who didn't give up on the development of Project R50.

Alex Moulton of Moulton Developments Limited – the man who designed the suspension for BMC's Mini, the founder of Hydrolastic and Hydragas suspension systems, and a friend of Issigonis himself – was particularly unimpressed with the new car. He was one of the first critics to argue that the MINI was far too big to be of the Mini bloodline. According to the press, he said:

> It's enormous. The original Mini was the best packaged car of all time. This is an example of how not to do it – it's huge on the outside and weighs the same as an Austin Maxi. The crash protection has been taken too far – I mean, what do you want, an armoured car? It is an irrelevance so far, as it has no part in the Mini history.

On the other hand, the legendary John Cooper was very impressed, later lending his name to the

ABOVE: **MINI UK showrooms
began to open across the
country in July 2001.** NEWSPRESS

RIGHT: **MINI celebrated its launch
year with a MINI Christmas tree
at the Tower of London.**
NEWSPRESS

The R50 MINI was launched as the entry-level One and sportier Cooper. MAGIC CAR PICS

performance model of the new MINI – the MINI Cooper S, John Cooper Works.

After forty-one years, the Mini was finally reincarnated. Little did the UK or even the world know that, while this car would make many enemies and allies upon its arrival to the market, the MINI would become a modern motoring legend, a car that would eventually win the hearts of thousands of motorists, and park proudly alongside the classic Mini we all adore, at hundreds of car shows across the globe.

The Mini to MINI story has been a hugely successful one, and no success story is founded without its scruples. Although many still remain sceptical, the majority of the members of true Mini fan clubs have accepted the new car. Visit any Mini-focused show and you'll sell a mix of both old and new. It may have caused one of the largest motoring conflicts in history, but when the R50 was launched in the year 2000, its purpose was never to replace the Mini: it was to continue its legacy.

The new MINI was gifted with a rather unique interior to match its outer styling. MAGIC CAR PICS

PART III

THE REINCARNATION OF BRITAIN'S SMALL CAR

CHAPTER SIX

BMW'S MINI POWERS INTO PRODUCTION

Since its launch in 2001, the MINI range has continued to expand. MAGIC CAR PICS

Since the MINI range became rather complex, it is probably best to give you a few quick facts regarding the many project codes BMW gave to their MINI cars. The first generation MINI, built between 2001 and 2006 (2007 in some markets), consisted of the One, the One D, the Cooper and the Cooper S model line-up. The One and the Cooper began production in 2001, ahead of the MINI Cooper S in 2002 and the One D in 2003. In July 2004, the first generation MINI received its first facelift, to coincide with the launch of the MINI Convertible. The facelifted MINIs received new head and rear light designs, a smoother grille with fewer slats and amended bumpers. The MINI Cooper, One and One D all shared the same internal project code of R50. Meanwhile the Cooper S was tagged R53, and the Convertible R52, even though it followed the Cooper S. These codes remained the same for all MINIs built before and after the facelift in 2004.

Launched in 2006, the second generation MINI was a major overhaul of the first MINI incarnation. Each and every external body panel was new, and the interior, although based on the same concept, had been completely remodelled. The second generation MINI, known as product R56, was launched in just two models: the Cooper and Cooper S, and the major difference was the fact that the new, new MINI had now inherited brand new engines made in the UK at BMW Plant Hams Hall. To the naked eye, the main visual differences consisted of a new headlight cluster, larger rear light clusters and a very different body shape to the MINI of 2001. The One and One D hatchbacks followed in early 2007, followed by the very first Clubman, R55, and a revised convertible, R57.

Despite the negative comments from anti-BMW MINI fans, the new MINI made it very difficult for people not to love it, especially the press. To worry that its status as a fashion accessory would damage its public appeal was a ridiculous notion, since the original car was exactly that: the endless photographs of models posing with Minis were evidential proof of this. Although it has since become a little

clichéd, the entry R50's set-up meant that the MINI does boast 'go-kart handling' qualities, firmly planted close to the tarmac and set up to hit every apex. The BMW wasn't 'mini' enough, but it was definitely 'Mini' enough. Up until May 2007, the first modern MINI – Project R50 – was bold, simple and symbolic.

In any case, it wasn't its looks that the automotive press was raving about: so much effort had gone into the development of the new car's chassis that they only had to experience what the MINI felt like powering through a corner to fall in love with it. In May 2001, *Autocar* magazine wrote in a review of the new MINI:

> *Far more interesting than the engine is the MINI's chassis, especially its ability to involve you in the action and even let you alter your cornering line using both throttle and steering. Yes, there's a hint of lift-off oversteer in extremis, but mostly there's so much grip that the only slip you're likely to encounter will be mild and at the front axle if you push really hard through a tight corner. This is a car you aim through corners confident that you're going to clip a blade of grass.*

Drivers were instantly impressed by the MINI's chassis and suspension set-up. MAGIC CAR PICS

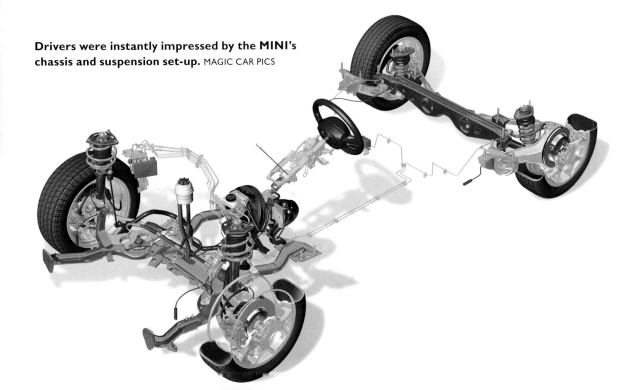

BMW MINI R50 One 1.6 3dr (2001 2006)

Layout and chassis
Three-door, four-seat hatchback with
  steel body/chassis
Transmission: SG5
Engine platform: W10B16 EU4
Engine layout: Transverse
Engine manufacturer: Chrysler
Double overhead camshaft (DOHC)

No. of doors: 3
No. of seats: 4

Engine
Type: 1.6-litre, in-line
No. of cylinders: 4
Valves: 16
No. of valves per cylinder: 4
Block material: Aluminium
Head material: Aluminium
Cooling: Air cooled
Fuel management: Siemens EMS 2000
Displacement: 1598cc
Stroke/Bore: 85.8/77mm
Power: 90bhp
Max. Torque: 140Nm
Compression ratio: 10.6:1

Transmission
Type: R56 5C35
1st 3.417
2nd 1.947
3rd 1.333
4th 1.054
5th 0.846

Suspension and steering
Suspension front: MacPherson struts, coil springs,
  anti-roll bar
Suspension rear: Z-axle, longitudinal struts, coil
  springs, anti-roll bar

Steering type: Rack and pinion EHPAS
Steering ratio: 13.18:1

Tyres
Tyre size front: 175/65R15 84 T
Tyre size rear: 175/65R15 84 T
Wheel size front: 5.5 J × 15 steel
Wheels size rear: 5.5 J × 15 steel

Brakes
Brake front and diameter: Ventilated discs 276×22mm
Brake rear and diameter: Solid discs 259×10mm

Dimensions
Vehicle length: 3,626mm (143in)
Vehicle width: 1,688mm (66in)
Vehicle height: 1,416 / 1,428mm (56/56in)
Wheelbase: 2,467mm (97in)
Turning circle: 10.66m (35ft)
Overhang front: 622mm (24in)
Overhang rear: 537mm (21in)
Track front: 1,458mm (57in)
Track rear: 1,466mm (58in)
Trunk volume: 150 litres
Tank capacity: 50 litres

Unladen weight: 1,065/1,140kg (2,348/2,514lb)
Axle load ratio, rear: 38.5 per cent
Gross vehicle weight: 1,495kg (3,296lb)
Payload: 430kg (948lb)
Axle load limit front: 870kg (1,918lb)
Axle load limit rear: 730kg (1,610lb)

Performance
Top speed: 112mph (180km/h)
Acceleration: 0–62mph: 10.7 seconds

Fuel consumption
Combined: 43mpg (6.6ltr/100km)
CO_2 emissions: 158g/km

The R50 MINI was launched in two versions: the entry-level One, and the sportier Cooper. Although the MINI was awarded top marks for its ability to stick to the tarmac in tight bends, it lost points for performance values. Even the Cooper didn't live up

to expectations. This was mostly due to the MINI's on-board Chrysler engine, which took the media by surprise, not quite making the cut for a sporty hot hatch in the earlier 2000s. *Autocar* continued:

> *With 116bhp and tipping the scales at a sporty 1,125kg, the MINI's sprinting ability slots it into warm-hatch territory. Good traction helps pull the car to 60mph in 9.3 seconds, but accelerating from 0–100mph takes a lengthy 28.4 seconds. Nor did the*

LEFT: **The MINI entry-level One may not have the power, but it did inherit the handling.** NEWSPRESS

BELOW: **The more powerful Cooper S came along in 2002, boasting 163bhp.** NEWSPRESS

BMW MINI R50 Cooper 1.6 3dr (2001–2006)

Layout and chassis
Three-door, four-seat hatchback with
    steel body/chassis
Transmission: SG5
Engine platform: W10B16 EU4
Engine layout: Transverse
Engine manufacturer: Chrysler
Double overhead camshaft (DOHC)

No. of doors: 3
No. of seats: 4

Engine
Type: 1.6-litre, in-line
No. of cylinders: 4
Valves: 16
No. of valves per cylinder: 4
Block material: Aluminium
Head material: Aluminium
Cooling: Air cooled
Fuel management: Siemens EMS 2000
Displacement: 1998cc
Stroke/Bore: 85.8/77mm
Power output: 115bhp
Max. torque: 149Nm
Compression ratio: 10.6:1

Transmission
Type: R56 5C39
1st 3.417
2nd 1.947
3rd 1.333
4th 1.054
5th 0.846
Reverse: 3.58
Final drive: 3.94

Suspension and steering
Suspension front: MacPherson struts, coil springs,
    anti-roll bar
Suspension rear: Z-axle, longitudinal struts, coil
    springs, anti-roll bar

Steering type: Rack and pinion EHPAS
Steering ratio: 13.18:1

Tyres
Tyre size front: 175/65R15 84 H
Tyre size rear: 175/65R15 84 H

Wheel size front: 5.5 J × 15 alloys
Wheels size rear: 5.5 J × 15 alloys

Brakes
Brake front and diameter: Ventilated discs 276×22mm
Brake rear and diameter: Solid discs 259×10mm

Dimensions
Vehicle length: 3,626mm (143in)
Vehicle width: 1,688mm (66in)
Vehicle height: 1,408/1,420mm (55/56in)
Wheelbase: 2,467mm (97in)
Turning circle: 10.66m (35ft)
Overhang front: 622mm (24in)
Overhang rear: 537mm (21in)
Track front: 1,458mm (57in)
Track rear: 1,466mm (58in)
Trunk volume: 150 litres
Tank capacity: 50 litres

Unladen weight: 1,075/1,150kg (2,370/2,536lb)
Axle load ratio, rear: 38.6 per cent
Gross vehicle weight: 1,505kg (3,319lb)
Payload: 430kg (948lb)
Axle load limit front: 870kg (1,918lb)
Axle load limit rear: 730kg (1,610lb)

Performance
Top speed: 124mph (200km/h)
Acceleration: 0–62mph: 8.9 seconds

Fuel consumption
City: 30.8mpg (9.2ltr/100km)
Motorway: 50.5mpg (5.6ltr/100km)
Combined: 41mpg (6.9ltr/100km)
CO_2 emissions: 168g/km

MINI enjoy the standard Autocar flexibility tests, and managed only a 9.7 seconds fourth gear 30–50mph time. A great lugger it is not. Thank over-tall gearing for that. Sure, the MINI has enough performance to make it fun, but it's not GTi; at least not in a straight line.

BMW did have a trick up its sleeve, though, and one that would provide the press with the power they had been craving. The Cooper S had been on the MINI development board long before it hit the road in 2002 as Project R53, with sketches by Frank Stephenson dating back to 1998. It was at the top of the MINI league table, ready to take on the likes of the Volkswagen Golf GTi with an Eaton supercharger bolted to the engine, which gave the little car a useful power surge to 163bhp. Any criticism that the MINI wasn't powerful enough was quite literally left behind in a cloud of tyre smoke, with the car now boasting a 2sec quicker 0–60mph time, as well as further enhanced chassis and braking modifications to make sure the car could handle the extra power and torque. In fact, when behind the wheel of a supercharged Cooper S – on 17in alloys – you can easily lose yourself in nostalgia from thinking you were driving the original 1275GT.

If the Cooper S wasn't enough to quench the average speed craver's thirst, then MINI's John Cooper Works conversion pack gave owners the opportunity to step up another peg, giving their MINIs an outstanding 210bhp. The John Cooper Works (JCW) performance pack was essentially an aftermarket conversion kit, but it was offered through authorized MINI dealerships, meaning that the option to upgrade was not only much more appealing than taking your car to the backstreets, it was also an easy process. Therefore, a great number of owners opted for the JCW configuration. The unique JCW exhaust system also meant the JCW MINI not only performed like a little pocket-rocket should: it sounded like one, too. *Autocar* came back with its tail between its legs; the leading automotive title appeared to adore the new performance MINI:

The Works offers extra willingness to rev and better throttle responses, but the matching

The John Cooper Works conversion kit pushed MINI horsepower up to 210bhp. MAGIC CAR PICS

of the extra performance with the revised MINI's gear ratios. It still needs working to extract its full potential, but you no longer suffer a trudge around the rev counter waiting for the power to arrive. It's now a gloriously frantic affair, goading you into driving in classic all-out Mini style. A louder exhaust complements the increased induction noise, although the supercharger scream dominates.

If Rover had got its way, the new MINI would have been powered by the K-Series unit. Yes, it was light and efficient to run, but the twin-cam block built at Longbridge wasn't easy to squeeze under the MINI's long bonnet. Instead, the new car was given a new heart, the new petrol engine known as a Tritec or Pentagon, created in a joint venture between Chrysler and BMW, and which, surprisingly, was more than capable of living up to its expectations. The engine is only offered in the form of a 1.6-litre with a 16-valve cylinder head, but boasts different power outputs for each MINI model. The entry-level One develops

AN OVERWHELMING START TO MINI PRODUCTION

The MINI was never going to be a new car far ahead of its time, like its predecessor. It was designed to be a conventional car that was accessible to all, but it was also engineered to ooze sporty characteristics and agility. Unlike the classic Mini of 1959, which was primarily designed to provide passenger comfort and the largest amount of interior space possible within the smallest exterior package, BMW's MINI focused on the achievements and motorsport heritage of the classic Cooper. Twenty-first-century buyers certainly weren't put off by this fact, and couldn't wait to be the proud owner of the new MINI. During the car's opening weekend in July 2001, more than 50,000 people visited the UK's 150 MINI dealerships to see the new One and Cooper models.

BMW Plant Oxford at Cowley saw production capacity quite literally rocket through the roof, and it remained that way throughout the first five years of production. More than 700,000 MINIs rolled off the production line between 2001 and 2006, proving that the MINI was just as successful five years into production as it was when it was first launched. The hatchback's residual values were unrivalled, with one-year-old cars collecting money for new car prices. It would only get better, too, since BMW chose 2006/2007 as the year to launch the second generation MINI, R56. The new version of the MINI retained a similar look to the original R50, R52 and R53 models and was based on the same foundations, only it was now entering the territory of becoming much more of a premium car.

Yet it was actually cheaper to build than the first generation MINI. Six years after the launch, MINI production reached 1,000,000.

LEFT: **In 2004, the 500,000th MINI was built at Plant Oxford.** NEWSPRESS

BELOW: **In 2007, this figure doubled as the millionth MINI was built at Plant Oxford.** NEWSPRESS

90bhp, while the Cooper and Cooper S churn out a more impressive 115bhp. The Cooper S also received a boost in power from its Eaton M45 supercharger, pushing its final performance figure up to 163bhp. The whine from the supercharger at the squeeze of the accelerator, at the time, was enough to win any petrol-head's heart, and that is still the case today.

On both the One and Cooper models, the 1.6-litre unit is mated to the Rover-derived R65 five-speed gearbox – more commonly known as the 'Midlands five-speed'. The Cooper S, on the other hand, received a six-speed Getrag box. One of the main weak points of the Mk1 (R50) MINI One and Cooper was the early gearbox failures of the 'Midland five-speed', especially when they were driven hard or underwent tuning programmes. When the MINI received a facelift in 2004 – and the MINI Convertible was launched – the MINI One and Cooper models also received stronger Getrag five-speed gearboxes, while the Cooper S continued to be fitted with the six-speed Getrag.

The front-mounted transverse configuration of the engine and gearbox was one of the key design challenges facing the MINI, due to the length of the bonnet. In order to meet Euro NCAP safety ratings, the engineers had to ensure maximum crash safety, and optimum configuration of the longitudinal members in the engine compartment were prioritized, posing an additional limit on the permitted length of the engine and gearbox. Depending on the spacing between the cylinders, the restriction on the powertrain determines how large or small the gearbox can be. This meant that a conventional two-shaft gearbox with the gears behind one another was never going to fit in the MINI's engine bay. Rover's decision to fit the R65 gearbox made perfect sense, not just because it was cheaper, but because it was more compact than the two-shaft layout and didn't suffer from inherent cyclic vibrations, and therefore didn't require a mass damper.

Originally designed by PSA (Peugeot-Citroen), the R65 was also easy enough to get hold of, since it was already being manufactured at the Longbridge site and was used in a number of Rover Group's front-wheel-drive cars. MINI product leader from 1996 to 1999, Chris Lee and his team persisted and eventually won the argument as to why the new MINI should feature the R65 box – but that didn't prevent it from going wrong. MINI's policy was to replace instead of repair when the gearboxes suffered a fatal deficit, leaving many R50 One and Cooper owners with hefty bills from MINI specialist service centres – which was good news for incoming business, but not so good for the owners. The first generation MINI was also offered with a CVT automatic gearbox, but this proved unpopular with drivers.

Beneath its retro yet innocent-looking styling, the MINI wasn't a soft touch – in fact, its suspension set-up was nothing short of genius. The front of the car was fitted with standard MacPherson struts and an anti-roll bar, but at the rear, the car was blessed with a rather costly multi-link Z-axle system. When the MINI first hit the roads, it was greatly admired for its unfailing handling. It was, and remains, a car that a driver can chuck into a corner and feel confident it will stick, which is mostly due to the Z-axle set-up. It would also explain why BMW didn't make any profit on the R50 One and Cooper models, since the system was rather premium for a car that was designed to offer value for money.

Stepping inside the car, it was clear that BMW strived to give the modern MINI a unique and admirable look, much like the classic. The key link between the original Mini of 1959 and the new BMW MINI of 2001 is the centralized speedometer and the rev-counter mounted on the steering column. Then there are those curvy storage compartments in the front passenger and driver's doors, which – as you will remember – resemble the hefty door holders designed by John Sheppard to store Issigonis's liquor to make his favourite Martini. That was always the key selling point for the Mini: a large car, cleverly packaged into a small shell. With that in mind, BMW focused on making sure the new hatch was a derivative of the original family car, but this time with higher quality materials and refinement. It wasn't perfect, though. In the early days, the MINI didn't boast the tightest of designs; the dash was often referred to as too 'plastic', as it suffered from a few squeaks and rattles, and occasionally things did fall off. But the desirable classic wasn't perfect, either. So perhaps this helped to pay homage to the original car's teething problems that we grew to love it for – much like the imperfections of a best friend or partner that we couldn't be without.

BMW MINI R53 Cooper S 1.6 3dr 2003 (2002–2006)

Layout and chassis

Three-door, four-seat hatchback with
steel body/chassis

Engine platform: W10B16 EU4
Transmission: SG5

No. of doors: 3
No. of seats: 4

Engine

Type: 1.6-litre, in-line, supercharged
No. of cylinders: 4
Valves: 16
No. of valves per cylinder: 4
Block material: Aluminium
Head material: Aluminium
Cooling: Air cooled
Fuel management: Siemens EMS 2000
Displacement: 1598cc
Stroke/Bore: 85.8/77mm
Power output: 163bhp
Max. torque: 210Nm
Compression ratio: 8.3:1

Transmission

Type: Getrag 285
1st 11.426
2nd 7.181
3rd 5.396
4th 4.408
5th 3.655
6th 2.986

Suspension and steering

Suspension front: MacPherson struts, coil springs,
anti-roll bar
Suspension rear: Z-axle, longitudinal struts, coil
springs, anti-roll bar

Steering type: Rack and Pinion EHPAS
Steering ratio: 13.8:1

Tyres

Tyre size front: 195/55R16 87 V
Tyre size rear: 195/55R16 87 V

Wheel size front: 6.5 J × 16 alloys run flat
Wheels size rear: 6.5 J × 16 alloys run flat

Brakes

Brake front and diameter: Ventilated discs 276×22mm
Brake rear and diameter: Solid discs 259×10mm

Dimensions

Vehicle length: 3,655mm (144in)
Vehicle width: 1,688mm (66in)
Vehicle height: 1,416/1,428in (56/56in)
Wheelbase: 2,467mm (97in)
Turning circle: 10.66m (35ft)
Overhang front: 647mm (25in)
Overhang rear: 541mm (21in)
Track front: 1,454mm (57in)
Track rear: 1,460mm (57in)
Luggage capacity: 150 litres
Tank capacity: 50 litres

Unladen weight: 1,140/1,215kg (2,514/2,679lb)
Axle load ratio, rear: 37.3 per cent
Gross vehicle weight: 1,570kg (3,462lb)
Payload: 430kg (948lb)
Axle load limit front: 890kg (1,962lb)
Axle load limit rear: 760kg (1,676lb)

Performance

Top speed: 135mph (217km/h)
Acceleration: 0–60mph: 7.2 seconds

Fuel consumption

Combined: 33mpg (8.6ltr/100km)
CO_2 emissions: 202g/km

ANOTHER FIRST FOR MINI

2003 was another milestone for the MINI, when BMW introduced the Toyota-powered MINI One D. The introduction of a diesel engine hugely broadened the appeal of the MINI, thus attracting a much wider target market, which perhaps required a slightly more economical hatchback for long-distance, everyday commutes, but one that could still be used as a fun car at the weekends with the same modern appearance. Producing 75bhp, the new power unit could offer a combined fuel consumption figure of 65mpg (4.3ltr/100km) (for lighter-footed owners), as well as a low tax bill, since it only emitted 117g/km of CO_2 emissions. The One D's economical qualities didn't compromise the little car's performance, though: it could still sprint from 0–60mph in a respectable 12.9sec and go on to reach a top speed of 110mph (177km/h) – impressive figures for a modest diesel hatchback.

After three years in production, and after the introduction of a diesel-powered One, BMW finally decided to send Project R52 – the hugely anticipated MINI Convertible – into production, marking the introduction of the very first body variation for the new MINI. By this point, MINI had suffered from a few teething problems, including a number of recalls, which didn't bode well in the early stages of its life.

In 2003, MINI introduced the Toyota-powered MINI One D. NEWSPRESS

ABOVE: **Three years into production, the MINI received its first facelift.** MAGIC CAR PICS

LEFT: **The Cooper S also received a surge in power in 2004, boasting 163bhp.** NEWSPRESS

But somehow it managed to redeem itself by simply being a MINI: it looked the part, it felt the part and it sounded the part, and most importantly, it made its owners enjoy driving it. This year also saw the entire range receive its first facelift, which consisted of a range of significant changes. It was given a slightly revised and restyled front end, as well as interior tweaks. One major alteration was underneath the bonnet, when BMW finally decided to drop the troublesome R65 gearbox from the entire range, and replaced it with five-speed Getrag boxes for both the One and Cooper.

The Cooper S also received a surge in power, jumping from 163bhp to 170bhp as standard. The arrival of the MINI Convertible was conveniently timed as the sales of soft-top cars were booming, so it was an important addition to the range. It wasn't slap-dash either; it featured a power-operated hood, which could also be conveniently partially retracted

to act as a sunroof for when drivers didn't fancy a bad hair day. As it turned out, UK motorists just couldn't get enough of the convertible, with sales rocketing by the end of 2004. Alongside the hatchback, in the form of a commuter (One D), run-around (One and Cooper) and sports car (Cooper S), the Convertible played a huge role in attracting a wealth of new customers. The two cars arguably accounted for the brand's early success in the small-car sector.

RIGHT: **The MINI Convertible became the UK's bestselling soft-top in 2006.** NEWSPRESS

BELOW: **The MINI Convertible overlooks Canary Wharf in London.** NEWSPRESS

A MODERN-DAY MASTERPIECE

Since its launch in 2001, the MINI has become the ultimate car for personalization and customization. It is said that the MINI range now features infinite specifications, ranging from colour schemes and optional extras to engines and tuning packs. Between the years 2001 and 2007, as the MINI brand was finding its ground, the line-up was relatively simple: the standard One, and the singing and dancing Cooper and Cooper S models for the more adventurous buyers. It remained that way when the diesel power unit came along in 2003, with the oil burner offered strictly in the One trim, and later when the Convertible was launched in Cooper and Cooper S form. While the model line-up appeared fairly straightforward, things got a little more complicated with the introduction of optional extras. It is a well known fact that BMW's marketing team was a mastermind at pricing the cars so that they fell in the 'reasonably priced' sector, before going on to present buyers with a hefty desirable options list, boosting appeal and with it, the overall price. It was a crafty plan, but it is certainly one that worked during that time. Option packs weren't new for the MINI: they had been in full swing since 2003 in order to maintain the strong levels of demand and offer a little something for everybody.

The MINI One was offered with the choice of a Salt or Pepper pack: these packs essentially stringed together a range of the popular optional extras, which customers would find themselves requesting individually anyway. In terms of simplicity, the fixed price packages were easy to understand and greatly sought after, in comparison to an intensely long list of extras, which could eventually be the reason behind buying a £20,000 MINI for £25,000. Salt was the cheaper of the two packs: it added items that you'd expect to come as standard, such as doormats, front fog lights and a rev-counter, while the £750 Pepper pack added more detail, such as 17in alloy wheels.

The MINI range now features infinite specifications, making every MINI unique.
NEWSPRESS

The Cooper and Cooper S models received relatively similar packages, only they were extended to include a range-topping Chilli pack, which included more performance upgrades such as more lavish, larger wheels and sports suspension.

The convertible MINI was available with the same option packs as the hardtops, although the base model price for the soft-top was significantly higher than the tin-tops, which explains why some MINI customers were spending almost £30,000 on a new MINI – quite a surreal figure, since the classic Mini was designed as a small budget family car. It looked as though the MINI of the twenty-first century was inching closer to a premium badge, with greater refinement, the latest gadgets and gizmos, better efficiency and more power.

But that's all before reaching the John Cooper model. Even though these models were essentially an aftermarket conversion, the JCW (known as the 'works' kit) could also be specced to meet the individual customer's requirements. Being the most powerful MINI of the range, the options mostly included performance upgrades, but the most significant alteration was its more powerful supercharger, which achieved the JCW's power output of 210bhp. The JCW was also fitted with a not-so-modest body kit, which focused on larger wheel arches and a larger front and rear bumper. The most extreme version was the MINI Cooper S JCW GP (GP1).

The John Cooper Works kit could produce a hefty 210bhp. NEWSPRESS

MINI's John Cooper Works kit offered larger alloys, more power and louder noise. NEWSPRESS

THE ULTIMATE PAIR

The first two generations of the John Cooper Works MINIs were viewed as the ultimate modern-day hot hatches: powerful, bold and noisy. That is until BMW took the term 'performance MINI' to a whole new level, by launching GP models of its more powerful cars. As well as adding more horsepower, the GP cars were kitted out with roll cages, rear spoilers and front splitters for more downforce, and were stripped to the metal to complete the 'race car' feel. The GP models even featured parts from the MINI Challenge race car, which compete in the one-make series. But only 2,000 examples of each model ever left the production line, making them just as desirable today as they were back then.

THE FASTEST MINI: THE MINI COOPER S JOHN COOPER WORKS GP KIT (GP1)

Launched in 2006, the Cooper S John Cooper Works GP kit (GP1) was limited to a production run of just 2,000 cars, and only 449 Cooper S JCW GP1s were destined to be sold in the UK – although according to GPMINI.net, only 437 GP1s actually found homes

here. BMW marketed the GP as a 'baby M car', giving the little car even more power, upgraded kit and a better chassis. Each car was even individually numbered, with its lucky figure(s) proudly displayed on the roof and on the dashboard. It was built as a 'body-in-white' car at the Oxford MINI Plant before being shipped to Bertone in Italy for final assembly, hand-finishing and painting.

The 1.6-litre power unit of the Cooper S, which has already proved it could be tuned to 210bhp for the standard JCW model, could now squeeze out an extra 8 horsepower, producing 218bhp and 245Nm of torque. This meant that the GP1 was propelled from 0–100km/h in under 6.5sec. Nevertheless, it wasn't cheap: its price tag was £2,880 more expensive than the Cooper S JCW it was based on, with an 'on the road' price of £22,000, making it difficult for buyers to justify the extra cash.

So why had BMW decided to produce the JCW GP Kit, over the regular 'works' package? It is said that Andreas Decher, leader of the chassis validation team, was extremely passionate about the MINI and what it stood for, much like John Cooper with the original Mini. His aim was to provide customers with the ultimate MINI, with no compromise (even if it meant losing the rear seats). In order to cope with the extra power, minimize torque steer and avoid understeer through the corners, the GP was given a

The John Cooper Works GP was the most extreme MINI to hit the roads. NEWSPRESS

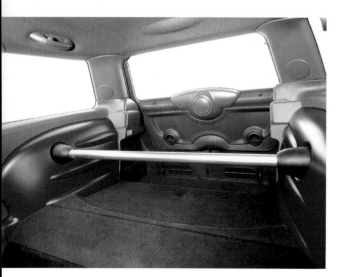

ABOVE: **The GP could stop just as quickly as it could pounce from 0 to 60mph.** NEWSPRESS

LEFT: **The GP was fitted with an aluminium strut-brace to help keep the car planted.** NEWSPRESS

Its remodelled front and rear bumpers, side skirts, underbody panelling and carbon fibre spoiler also made it instantly recognizable, while primarily helping to improve the car's aerodynamics. Fitted with exclusive, lightweight 18in alloy wheels and a set of JCW brakes, the GP could stop just as quickly as it could pounce from 0–60mph, and handled like a dream on the road. In place of the rear seats, the GP received a flat loading platform and was fitted with an aluminium strut-brace, helping to keep the car firmly planted on the tarmac and the rear more predictable when powering through corners. It may have been raw and stripped back to the metal, but the GP did receive a few luxuries, including Recaro heated leather seats and a three-spoke, multifunction sports steering wheel, on which the radio and cruise-control settings could be altered. Even today, eight years on, the MINI GP1 manages to retain impressive residual values, with a solid average after-sale price of £12,000.

larger intercooler than the Cooper S JCW, and a limited slip differential as standard. The standard steel R53 rear-axle trailing arms were also removed, and replaced with lighter and stiffer aluminium units. As well as removing the rear seats, the GP didn't get a rear window wiper, either – not particularly convenient since water seems to suction to the rear of the car on rainy days. BMW took weight reduction to the extreme.

The GP could, and still can be, clearly identified by its Thunder Blue paintwork, exclusive to the range, with a Pure Silver roof and Chilli Red mirror caps.

CHAPTER SEVEN

A MINI FOR THE NEXT GENERATION

In September 2006, production began on the new MINI R56 hatchback. NEWSPRESS

The second generation MINI received a number of styling upgrades. NEWSPRESS

The summer of 2006 marked the end of production for the first generation MINI hatch, which had now put the brand firmly on the map. By September, production of the second generation MINI hatchback, R56, had begun in Cooper and Cooper S form, but it wasn't until March 2007 that the new MINI One and One D followed on the production lines. The press feared that BMW had taken the fun out of the MINI, with ever-growing efficiency and safety regulations altering the development of the cars. Could R56 live up to the standards already set by R50, R53 and R52? It was clear that three key areas remained the same: the 'retro styling', the 'kart-like handling' and the 'wheel-at-each-corner control'.

What was so remarkable about the Mini, Mini Cooper and Mini Cooper S of the 1960s and 1970s was that on those 10in wheels, the little car really did handle like a go-kart. As the driver, the steering wheel connects you directly with the roads: you could feel everything those wheels were doing without any technologically enhanced systems such as power steering and anti-lock brakes (ABS) getting in the way. The Mini was raw and simple. By 2007 times had obviously changed, but MINI managed to retain those key driving qualities. Despite running on larger 15in, 16in and 17in wheels, the MINI is still one of the few hot hatches on the road to offer the same levels of handling and driver entertainment as its predecessor.

BMW MINI R56 One (2006–2015)

Layout and chassis
Three-door, four-seat hatchback with
  steel body/chassis

Engine platform: N12B14
Transmission: M6

No. of doors: 3
No. of seats: 4

Engine
Type: 1.6-litre, in-line
No. of cylinders: 4
Valves: 16
No. of valves per cylinder: 4
Block material: Aluminium
Head material: Aluminium
Cooling: Air cooled
Fuel management: MEV 17.2
Displacement: 1397cc
Stroke/Bore: 75.0/77.0mm
Power output: 96bhp
Max. Torque: 153Nm
Compression ratio: 11:1

Transmission
Type: Getrag G255
1st 3.214
2nd 1.792
3rd 1.194
4th 0.914
5th 0.784
6th 0.683

Suspension and steering
Suspension front: MacPherson struts, coil springs,
  anti-roll bar
Suspension rear: Z-axle, longitudinal struts, coil
  springs, anti-roll bar

Steering type: Rack and pinion Zahnst (EPS)
Steering ratio: 14.1:1

Tyres
Tyre size front: 175/65R15 84 H
Tyre size rear: 175/65R15 84 H

Wheel size front: 5.5 J × 15 steel wheel
Wheels size rear: 6.5 J × 16 steel wheel

Brakes
Brake front and diameter: Ventilated discs 280mm
Brake rear and diameter: Solid discs 259mm

Dimensions
Vehicle length: 3,699mm (146in)
Vehicle width: 1,683mm (66in)
Vehicle height: 1,407mm (55in)
Wheelbase: 2,467mm (97in)
Turning circle: 10.7m (35ft)
Overhang front: 565mm (22in)
Overhang rear: 139mm (5in)
Track front: 1,459mm (57in)
Track rear: 1,467mm (58in)
Trunk volume: 160–680cu m
Tank capacity: 40 litres

Unladen weight: 1,060/1,135kg (2,337/2,503lb)
Axle load ratio, rear: 38.9 per cent
Gross vehicle weight: 1,510kg (3,330lb)
Payload: 450kg (992lb)
Axle load limit front: 850kg (1,874lb)
Axle load limit rear: 740kg (1,632lb)

Performance
Top speed: 116mph (187km/h)
Acceleration 0–62mph: 10 seconds

Fuel consumption
Combined: 52mpg (5.4ltr/100km)
CO_2 emissions: 127g/km

NEW YEAR, NEW ENGINE: MINI MINIMALISM

There was more output, more efficiency and more driving fun thanks to a thoroughly revised range of petrol engines for the MINI, MINI Clubman and MINI Convertible. In 2010, the Hatchback, Clubman and Convertible were given an extensively revised range of petrol engines, with the key aim to make MINI the market leader in producing sporty yet efficient engines for premium small cars. From this point, all petrol MINIs would meet the EU5 exhaust emissions standard in Europe. The powertrain modifications further enhanced the relationship between performance and CO_2 emissions in all petrol-engined MINIs. The Cooper S, for example, was given a new 184bhp, 1.6-litre 4-cylinder engine, which emits only 136g/km of CO_2 per kilometre, according to the EU test cycle – that's 13g/km less than its predecessor.

The new MINI One MINIMALISM line, which was available with two engine variants, had the lowest emissions values of any petrol MINI, using optimized engine technology, brake energy regeneration, the auto start-stop function, shift point display and other MINIMALISM measures to achieve a CO_2 figure of 119g/km. In the new MINI petrol units, measures such as reducing friction and improving heat management in the basic engine enabled further improvements in efficiency. The engines were now served by a map-controlled oil pump with need-based operation, which ensures efficient use of energy.

Driving the more powerful Cooper S, the new 1.6-litre also featured another unique attribute in the small car segment: it was the first time that the twin-scroll turbocharger and petrol direct-injection system had been offered, together with fully variable valve control. Based on the 'Valvetronic' system

MINI introduced a new engine to the range, combining power with greater efficiency.
NEWSPRESS

used in BMW engines, this throttle-free load-control technology optimizes the engine's responses and enables a significant reduction in fuel consumption and emissions. It does so by adjusting the lift and opening period of the intake valves to the driver's power requirements within fractions of a second. The new engine was labelled the world's most efficient unit in this displacement class.

For those who are not hardcore MINI fans, it may have been slightly difficult to pinpoint the differences between the first and second generation cars. To look at, the two were very similar in appearance, and it looked as though the MINI had just been given another facelift. Considering how successful the first generation MINI had been, it made perfect sense to leave the shell mostly untouched, making only small amendments to its detail; the new MINI's looks were, after all, a key selling point and were unrivalled – although BMW assured the press that every panel was different and was based on a re-engineered platform. The new, new MINI featured a lower glass line as well as an extended rear window. The front headlights were another surprise: they were now mounted to the body, having previously been integrated in the bonnet.

BMW MINI R56 Cooper (2006–2015)

Layout and chassis
Three-door, four-seat hatchback with
   steel body/chassis

Engine platform: N12B14
Transmission: M6

No. of doors: 3
No. of seats: 4

Engine
Type: 1.6-litre, in-line
No. of cylinders: 4
Valves: 16
No. of valves per cylinder: 4
Block material: Aluminium
Head material: Aluminium
Cooling: Air cooled
Fuel management: MEV 17,2
Displacement: 1,598cc
Stroke/Bore: 85.8/77mm
Power output: 120bhp
Max. torque: 160Nm
Compression ratio: 11:1

Transmission
Type: Getrag G255
1st 3.214
2nd 1.792
3rd 1.194
4th 0.914
5th 0.784
6th 0.683
Reverse: 3.143
Final Drive: 4.35

Suspension and steering
Suspension front: MacPherson struts, coil springs,
   anti-roll bar
Suspension rear: Z-axle, longitudinal struts, coil
   springs, anti-roll bar

Steering type: Rack and Pinion Zahnst (EPS)
Steering ratio: 14.1:1

Tyres
Tyre size front: 175/65R15 84 H
Tyre size rear: 175/65R15 84 H
Wheel size front: 5.5 J × 15 light alloys
Wheels size rear: 6.5 J × 16 alloys run flat

Brakes
Brake front and diameter: Ventilated discs 280mm
Brake rear and diameter: Solid discs 259mm

Dimensions
Vehicle length: 3,699mm (146in)
Vehicle width: 1,683mm (66in)
Vehicle height: 1,407mm (55in)
Wheelbase: 2,467mm (97in)
Turning circle: 10.7m (35ft)
Overhang front: 565mm (22in)
Overhang rear: 139mm (5in)
Track front: 1,459mm (57in)
Track rear: 1,467mm (58in)
Trunk volume: 160–680cu m
Tank capacity: 40 litres

Unladen weight: 1,056/1,140kg (2,328/2,514lb)
Axle load ratio, rear: 38.7 per cent
Gross vehicle weight: 1,515kg (3,340lb)
Payload: 450kg (992lb)
Axle load limit front: 855kg (1,885lb)
Axle load limit rear: 740kg (1,632lb)

Performance
Top speed: 126mph (203km/h)
Acceleration: 0–60mph: 8.8 seconds

Fuel consumption
Combined: 52mpg (5.4ltr/100km)
CO_2 emissions: 239g/km

Inside the car, the MINI felt much more premium, with a high-quality feel to the cabin and a range of new gadgets and gizmos. The central speedometer still dominated the cockpit, as it always had done, only now it was bigger and featured integrated controls for the audio system. The interior ambiance could also be adapted to the mood via a switch that controlled the ambient lighting, which had a variety of colours. The new car was roomier, too.

Finally, because this last incarnation of the MINI was born at a time when fuel prices were rocketing once again, and vehicle tax bands continued to multiply figures for vehicles producing more than 120g/km of CO_2, it also boasted a number of efficiency credentials. By this point, MINI had been injected with a range of technological upgrades; it now featured a stop-start system, which shuts down the engine when the car is stopped for more than five seconds, and automatically restarts when the driver re-engages the clutch.

Underneath the metal, the MINI's slightly larger body could accommodate a range of new engines and a standard six-speed manual gearbox. To replace the Chrysler-built unit that powered the first generation MINI, BMW introduced a brand new 1.6-litre, 4-cylinder engine that was engineered at BMW's Hams Hall engine plant in Warwickshire. This particular power unit – known as the Prince engine – had been developed by BMW in conjunction with Peugeot-Citroën, with the base model Cooper running a normally aspirated version, featuring BMW's Valvetronic throttle system, which produced 118bhp. At the top of the range, the Cooper S was powered by a turbocharged version of the 4-cylinder engine, only without the Valvetronic system. Instead, it gained a direct injection, which enabled it to produce 173bhp and 259Nm of torque. For drivers wishing to feel a little sportier behind the wheel, the Cooper and Cooper S models also came with optional Aisin Warner automatic transmission, which could also be paired with paddle-shifters on the steering wheel.

Then of course there is the Cooper S John Cooper Works unit, capable of producing 210bhp and powering you from 0 to 100km/h in less than 7sec, and then going on to reach 146mph (235km/h). But was the turbocharged unit as liberating as the former supercharged Cooper S? It may not have sounded as good, but it was certainly more advanced. The engine in question features low controlled oil and water pumps, which automatically shut down to save energy when they are not in use. Meanwhile, the twin-scroll design turbocharger – featuring two separate channels of exhaust gas from two cylinders in order to reduce turbo-lag – helped to improve the MINI's top speed output. BMW strived to maintain the MINI's bottom-end grunt, while improving the car's top-end response. It certainly worked, and the peak 240Nm of torque is available all the way from 1,600 to 5,000rpm, with an 'overboost' to 260Nm available at an extra squeeze of the accelerator for overtaking. It may have lost the whine from the supercharger, but the 4-cylinder exhaust note certainly paired well with the sound of squealing rubber. In any case, for more relaxed, long distance commutes, the loss of the supercharger could be seen as a blessing, reducing cabin noise.

Talking of squealing, the second generation MINI also waved goodbye to that problematic electro-hydraulic steering set-up, which was replaced by electric power assistance. This didn't cause any dramas when it came to steering feel and handling: the wheel remained nicely weighted, and cornering responses were arguably improved. The adjustable chassis also played a significant role in the enjoyable cornering antics, with the DSC stability control system stepping in to prevent too much oversteer and the optional limited slip differential curing any signs of understeer. But with the flick of a switch, the traction control can be turned off and the rear of the car is firmly in the hands of the driver, opening up all sorts of possibilities for tail-happy fun. This is quite spectacular, considering the usual limitations of front-wheel-drive chassis.

To help tame the extra power and occasional cornering antics, the MINI was also fitted with larger discs, which would bring it to a halt rather rapidly. It is no wonder that the Cooper S can lap the legendary, notorious Nürburgring Nordschelieffe no less than 15sec quicker than the previous R53 Cooper S. The second generation MINI was so popular that it helped MINI production reach 1 million at Plant Oxford in April 2007.

DIESEL GETS SERIOUS

The second generation MINI One was added to the range early in 2007, followed by the introduction of the very first diesel-powered Cooper in April, labelled the Cooper D. Powered by a 1.6-litre engine, the diesel-powered unit would later – in 2011 – become available with a 2.0-litre unit for the automatic Cooper and a high performance diesel, the Cooper SD. The Cooper SD variant was launched across the Hatch, Convertible, Clubman and Countryman range and featured a 2-litre common-rail turbo-diesel engine, derived from MINI's existing 1.6-litre diesel unit, which already produced 141bhp and 305Nm of torque. The new 2-litre unit features an all-aluminium crankcase and a variable intake turbocharger, in addition to the full suite of MINI's MINIMALISM technology kit, which incorporates brake energy generation, auto stop/start and electric power steering.

As well as delivering an impressive 65.7mpg (4.3ltr/100km), the SD hatchback can still reach 0–100km/h in just over 8sec. The Clubman and Convertible versions weren't too far off, with an 8.6 and 8.7sec 0–100km/h time, and combined fuel consumption figures of 64.2mpg (4.4ltr/100km) and

62.8mpg (4.5ltr/100km). The larger Countryman was the least agile and least economical, with the front-wheel-drive Cooper SD reaching 62mph (100km/h) in 9.3sec, 1sec quicker than the ALL4 derivative, and delivered 61.4mpg (4.6ltr/100km). From a visual perspective, the Cooper SD aims to resemble that of the sporty Cooper S, sharing the larger front air intakes, the bonnet scoop and the roof spoiler (aside from the Convertible). Much like the petrol-powered Cooper S cars, the SD was rather pricey, starting from £18,750 for the hatchback and £23,190 for the Countryman ALL4.

ABOVE: **The SD features a 2.0-litre common-rail turbo-diesel engine, producing 141bhp.** NEWSPRESS

LEFT: **The SD resembles the sporty Cooper S, sharing larger front air intakes and the bonnet scoop.** NEWSPRESS

BMW MINI R56 Cooper S 3dr (2006–2015)

Layout and chassis
Three-door, four-seat hatchback with
    steel body/chassis

Engine platform: N12B14
Transmission: M6

No. of doors: 3
No. of seats: 4

Engine
Type: 1.6-litre, in-line, turbocharged
No. of cylinders: 4
Valves: 16
No. of valves per cylinder: 4
Block material: Aluminium
Head material: Aluminium
Cooling: Air cooled
Fuel management: MED 17,2
Displacement: 1598cc
Stroke/Bore: 85.8/77mm
Nominal power: 181bhp
Max. torque: 260Nm
Compression ratio: 10.5:1

Transmission
Type: Getrag G253
1st 3.308
2nd 2.13
3rd 1.483
4th 1.139
5th 0.949
6th 0.816

Suspension and steering
Suspension front: MacPherson struts, coil springs,
    anti-roll bar
Suspension rear: Z-axle, longitudinal struts, coil
    springs, anti-roll bar

Steering type: Rack and pinion Zahnst (EPS)
Steering ratio: 14.1:1

Tyres
Tyre size front: 195/55R16 87 V RSC
Tyre size rear: 195/55R16 87 V RSC
Wheel size front: 6.5 J × 16 light alloys
Wheels size rear: 6.5 J × 16 alloys run flat

Brakes
Brake front and diameter: Ventilated discs 294mm
Brake rear and diameter: Solid discs 259mm

Dimensions
Vehicle length: 3,714mm (146in)
Vehicle width: 1,683mm (66in)
Vehicle height: 1,407mm (55in)
Wheelbase: 2,467mm (97in)
Turning circle: 10.7m (35ft)
Overhang front: 565mm (22in)
Overhang rear: 130mm (5in)
Track front: 1,453mm (57in)
Track rear: 1,461mm (58in)
Luggage capacity: 160–680cu m
Tank capacity: 50 litres

Curb weight: 1,130/1,205kg (2,492/2,657lb)
Axle load ratio, rear: 37.8 per cent
Gross vehicle weight: 1,580kg (3,484lb)
Payload: 450kg (992lb)
Axle load limit front: 855kg (1,885lb)
Axle load limit rear: 755kg (1,665lb)

Performance
Top speed: 142mph
Acceleration: 0–60mph: 6.8 seconds

Fuel consumption
Combined: 48mpg (5.9ltr/100km)
CO_2 emissions: 136g/km

FLASHBACKS TO THE PAST

The MINI Clubman – A 'Mini' Estate

2007 was also the year that MINI decided it was time to follow in the footsteps of its predecessor and launch another brand new model to join the MINI line-up. Alongside the hatch and the convertible, MINI unveiled the Clubman, R55, which went on sale across Europe towards the end of the year in November. By this point, the MINI badge was sold in more than seventy countries worldwide, reaffirming MINI's importance in the modern automotive industry. You'll remember that 'Clubman' was the name given to the classic of the 1970s, which resulted in a square-fronted hot hatch, later developed into a practical estate car and the 1275GT hot hatch.

Being an estate car, the new MINI Clubman isn't based on the name it shares with the original, but on foundations laid by the Austin and Morris Mini Traveller and Countryman. Since BMW didn't own the rights to those names, the car maker christened its new estate car 'Clubman', which was essentially the same car as the hatchback, available in One, Cooper, Cooper S, Cooper D and JCW form, but with a longer tail. The Clubman is identical to the three-door hatchback from the B-pillar forward, while it features an overall length increased by 238.7mm (9.4in), a 78.7mm (3.1in) longer wheelbase, much more rear legroom and 260ltr (9.2cu ft) of extra space in the boot, which amounts to a 920ltr (33cu ft) luggage space with the rear seats folded. Unlike its three-door counterpart, the Clubman's rear space was its key selling point, with access via its rear bi-parting split doors. The Clubman also features bi-parting side doors, coined the Clubdoor. BMW also released the Clubman in a special edition Clubman Bond Street, named after the prestigious shopping venue in London.

In 2007, MINI launched the all-new Clubman variant – the modern MINI estate.
NEWSPRESS

The Clubman is based on the foundations laid by the Traveller and Countryman.
NEWSPRESS

RIGHT: **The Clubman features 260ltr (9.2cu ft) of extra luggage space in the boot.** NEWSPRESS

BELOW: **The Clubman is available in One, Cooper, S, SD and JCW form with bi-parting split doors.** NEWSPRESS

BOTTOM: **MINI released the Clubman Bond Street in 2013, after the prestigious shopping venue.** NEWSPRESS

The Convertible – Top-down Adventures

In 2008, BMW announced plans to launch a second generation Convertible – R57 – which, aside from running the new 4-cylinder engines and riding on a new suspension, benefited from a 10 per cent stiffer structure, preventing the rattles and shakes often experienced in the former R52 Convertible. Hitting the showroom in March 2009, the Convertible was available in the usual Cooper and Cooper S forms, with the John Cooper Works version appearing a little later into the future. The new Convertible featured a raised shoulder line, highlighted with a chrome strip. The Cooper and Cooper S models retained the traditional hexagonal radiator grille with round headlights, while the Cooper S also received its usual 20mm (¾in) high 'powerdome' bonnet scoop, a gaping front air intake and a rear bumper incorporating a large diffuser and twin, centrally mounted exhaust pipes.

ABOVE: **In 2008, BMW announced plans to launch a second generation convertible – R57.** NEWSPRESS

LEFT: **The Convertible benefited from a 10 per cent stiffer structure, preventing the rattles often experienced in the former R52.** NEWSPRESS

RIGHT: **The electric roof can be lowered and raised in just 15sec at speeds of up to 20mph (32km/h).** NEWSPRESS

BELOW: **The Openometer records how many hours the owner spends driving with the roof down.** NEWSPRESS

The new Convertible's powertrains were inherited from the outgoing Mini hatchback, which benefited from the MINI version of BMW's Efficient Dynamics systems known as MINIMALISM. The system includes features such as auto start-stop, brake energy regeneration and shift point display, and can improve fuel economy and CO_2 emissions by up to 23 per cent. This resulted in the new Cooper and Cooper S Convertibles being two VED bands lower than their predecessors, while still pumping out an impressive 120 and 175bhp. With an aim of reducing scuttle shake, the new Convertible's body structure, floorpan, A-pillars and side sills were also revised and strengthened, which also improved crash protection and reduced bodyweight by 10kg (22lb). Small highlights included the fact that the electric roof could be lowered and raised in just 15sec at speeds of up to 20mph (32km/h), as well as partially retracted at speeds of up to 75mph (120km/h), to act as a sunroof, and these were features that made the new

Convertible such a hit. Its boot capacity had even been increased by 5ltr (0.2cu ft) to 125ltr (4.4cu ft) with the roof down, and 170ltr (6.0cu ft) with the roof up. Similarly, for drivers who didn't often carry rear passengers, the rear seats could be folded to increase the boot capacity to a total of 660ltr (23.3cu ft) – not bad for a topless, sporty run-around.

The best feature has to be its Openometer, which records how many hours the owner spends driving with the roof down, leaving them with no excuse but to keep that roof off. To make sure the new Convertible stood out as a MINI marvel in its own right, it was launched with two new colours, exclusive to the model: Interchange Yellow and Horizon Blue – not what you would call subtle – with the roof colours remaining basic with Black, Denim Blue and Hot Chocolate. Prices were beginning to creep up, though, with the entry level Cooper starting from £15,995 and the Cooper S jumping to £18,995, and while air conditioning was now standard, those pricey yet desirable optional extras were bound to add at least another £2,000 to the list price.

To mark the brand's fiftieth birthday, more than 25,000 people from forty countries arrived at the Silverstone Circuit for a three-day festival of cars, MINI Challenge racing and music. More than 10,000 classic Minis and modern MINIs lined up alongside each other to mark this joyous and historic occasion, and amongst the visitors were the original cars from *The Italian Job* movie, as well as the model created by British fashion designer Paul Smith in 1997. For BMW this day was the perfect opportunity to reveal three new fiftieth anniversary models in honour of

ABOVE LEFT: **To celebrate the brand's fiftieth anniversary, BMW launched three new MINI models: the 50 Camden...** NEWSPRESS

ABOVE: **...the 50 Mayfair...**

LEFT: **...and John Cooper Works Championship 50.** NEWSPRESS

the mighty Mini, to which it owed its success: the MINI 50 Camden, the MINI 50 Mayfair and the MINI John Cooper Works Championship 50.

The 50 Camden and 50 Mayfair hatches went on sale for just one year in September 2009, and were available in Cooper, Cooper D and Cooper S form. The 50 Camden could be identified by its solid white roof, coupled with either White Silver, Midnight Black or Horizon Blue metallic paintwork, and White Shield 17in alloy wheels. The 50 Mayfair was available in a combination of either Hot Chocolate or Midnight

Black metallic paintwork with a White roof, or Pepper White solid paintwork with a Black roof with unique 17in, twelve-spoke Infinity Stream alloy wheels and toffee leather seats. The two cars certainly carried a unique style, as well as a rather hefty price tag: the 50 Camden ranged from £18,615 to £21,030, while the 50 Mayfair was priced from £18,415 to £21,280.

But it was the limited edition JCW Championship 50 model that was extra special. Conceived by John Cooper's son, Mike Cooper, the car was designed to commemorate the achievements of his late father, as well as his business Cooper Car Company Ltd; he won both the Formula 1 Drivers' and Constructors' Championships with Jack Brabham in 1959 – the year the Mini was launched. The production run was limited to just 250 examples, solely destined for Europe. All the cars were finished in Connaught Green with Jet Black 17in cross-spoke alloy wheels.

MINI-E: IT'S ELECTRIC

In 2009, the UK launch of the MINI-E was overseen by Lord Drayson, Minister of Science and Innovation, Andy Hearn, general manager at MINI UK, and Lord Adonis, Secretary of State for Transport. It all began when the government's Technology Strategy Board – with a key responsibility to promote business innovation in technology – announced a consortium lead by BMW Group that would be supported by a proportion of a £25m fund. This enabled the electric MINI to be tested on British roads by public sector, private and corporate drivers before the end of the year. The objective of the Technology Strategy Board was to encourage manufacturers to develop ultra-low carbon vehicles and bring them to market. The trial was part of MINI's commitment to MINIMALISM, in which the brand has now completed two phases of official public field trials. The MINI-E test programme was the UK's most in-depth trial ever to take place, while BMW Group became the first to use lithium-ion

technology in an all-electric vehicle to operate on the road. The development continues, and BMW Group, using the MINI badge, aims to shape the future of cars.

It all started in the winter of 2009, with the arrival of the MINI-E in the UK. The selected number of electric MINIs were deployed for daily use within a test area in the south-east of England and were on the road for twelve months, where they were trialled to evaluate the technical and social aspects of living with a 100 per cent electric car, and more importantly a fully electric MINI, in a real-world environment. The MINI-E UK Research Consortium, of which BMW Group was the lead partner, comprised several organizations based around Oxford and the south-east of England, all of which played vital roles in the collaborative trial. Members of the consortium included the electric energy and infrastructure provider, Scottish and Southern Energy, and academic partner, Oxford Brookes University's Sustainable Vehicle Engineering Centre. Scottish and Southern Energy were responsible for the infrastructure of the field trial by installing charging points for all MINI-E test vehicles. The trial came to an end in March 2011.

The MINI-E was powered by state-of-the-art lithium-ion, 35kWh battery packs, which are air-cooled and monitored separately and take approximately four to five hours to charge. The MINI-E can produce 150kW of power, 220Nm of torque, and can accelerate from 0–100km/h in 8.5sec before reaching

In 2009, the MINI-E joined the Government electric vehicle announcement.
NEWSPRESS

ABOVE: **The MINI-E was tested on British roads by the British public on a daily basis.** NEWSPRESS

LEFT: **The MINI-E was powered by state-of-the-art lithium-ion, 35kW battery packs.** NEWSPRESS

an electronically limited top speed of 95mph (153km/h). In ideal driving conditions, the E can achieve a driving range of 155 miles (250km), but this is limited to between 80 and 110 miles (129 and 177km) in normal conditions, which includes traffic, road surface changes and speed variants. The MINI-E is also packed with standard equipment including dynamic stability control (DSC), 16in alloy wheels, a sports leather steering wheel, sports seats, air conditioning, and cloth/leather upholstery in Carbon Black with yellow stitching. The MINI-E can easily be identified by its E decals. Being a MINI, even if it is powered by electricity, the E still benefits from the signature 50/50 weight balance ratio, tuned suspension and 'wheels all-the-way-at-the-corners' attributes, meaning that it can deliver the same nimble handling for which its petrol- and diesel-powered cousins are renowned.

CHAPTER EIGHT

THE SPECIAL EDITIONS

In February 2011 MINI released a new option Sport Pack, based on the John Cooper Works conversion, which was available on the Hatch and Convertible models. The pack featured an aerodynamic package, which included unique front and rear aprons and a honeycomb mesh over the main air intake. Inside, Sport Pack cars received the same black leather sports steering wheel as the JCW, cloth/leather sports seats and Piano Black trim, as well as lightweight 17in JCW cross-spoke alloy wheels. The Sport Pack was also fitted with dynamic traction control and electronic differential lock control, further improving the car's handling and enhancing driver engagement. The

Sport Pack wasn't exactly a quick bolt-on, however, and it came at a price, starting from £2,150 for the MINI One and rising to £2,995 for the Mini Cooper and Cooper D Convertible. In the UK, MINI also announced two special edition cars: the MINI Clubman Hampton and the MINI Pimlico.

These two cars were to promote a new customization programme called MINI Yours, which further enhanced the MINI's ever-growing range of customization options; it would be on sale for just twelve months. The Clubman Hampton was finished in bespoke Reef Blue metallic paint with a Silver roof, rear door surrounds and Damson Red detailing. All Clubman

In 2011, BMW announced two special MINI editions: the Clubman Hampton and the Pimlico. NEWSPRESS

Hamptons were fitted with MINI's Chilli Pack, and 17in, twin-spoke alloy wheels. For the entry-level Cooper version of the Clubman Hampton you'd be looking at a £20,360 price tag, while the Cooper SD jumped to £23,185. The hatch-only MINI Pimlico came in a much more vibrant Laser Blue metallic paint finish, which was originally only available on the Cooper S and JCW cars. It was also fitted with 16in JCW, twin-spoke alloy wheels, and featured a Piano Black interior. The MINI Pimlicos were priced a little cheaper, starting at £14,465 for the MINI One.

'MINI INSPIRED BY GOODWOOD'

Continuing to add to its string of limited and special edition models, in April 2011 the most luxurious MINI ever to be produced was unveiled: 'MINI Inspired by Goodwood' was limited to a production run of 1,000 cars, which were built under the watchful eye of BMW Group's partner company and British premium car maker, Rolls-Royce. Powered by the same 1.6-litre, 184bhp turbocharged engine that powers the Cooper S, the premium-packaged MINI was a mini Rolls-Royce. The Goodwood edition was rather modest in its appearance, so unless you are a red hot MINI fanatic, you would have to look twice. The trim colours, equipment and detailing were all decided by Alan Sheppard of Rolls-Royce design. Unlike the other MINI models, the Goodwood edition received a specifically selected central console, air vents, carpets, lounge leather seats, roof lining, door and interior cladding materials, all of which were finished in the carmaker's Cornsilk colouring. In addition, the dashboard and door-handle surfaces – manufactured at Goodwood – are finished in the typical and traditional premium wood trim, Walnut Burr, exclusive to Rolls-Royce.

The 'MINI Inspired by Goodwood' was also crammed with a range of technical gadgets, including Xenon adaptive headlights, park distance control, automatic air conditioning, and the MINI's audio

'MINI Inspired by Goodwood' was the most luxurious MINI ever made. NEWSPRESS

The Goodwood MINI was built under the watchful eye of British premium carmaker, Rolls-Royce.
NEWSPRESS

system, radio MINI visual boost, which features the Harman Kardon hi-fi speaker kit. To achieve a striking yet tasteful appearance, the 'MINI Inspired by Goodwood' was finished in metallic Diamond Black, exclusive to Rolls-Royce, which is highlighted by 17in lightweight, multi-spoke alloy wheels. Following BMW's announcement that the Goodwood MINI was on its way, the car made its debut at the Shanghai Motor Show, which is also when the brand dropped the price-related bomb: this little car was destined to receive a £40,000 price tag.

THE MINI COUNTRYMAN, R60

The MINI Countryman R60 was announced in January 2010. As MINI's first Crossover SUV (Sports Utility Vehicle) – not to mention the first five-door MINI model to be launched in BMW's era – it caused quite a stir; however, although it bears the historical 'Countryman' name, the new, five-door variation is a completely different car to that of the wood-trimmed estate car of the 1960s. Built at BMW's plant at Magna Steyr in Austria, the SUV is offered in a choice of two- or four-wheel-drive (known as ALL4), and is powered by the same 1.6-litre 4-cylinder petrol or 2.0-litre 4-cylinder diesel engines in the hatchback or Clubman, which can be paired to a six-

speed manual or a six-speed automatic gearbox (the automatic is not available on the entry-level One). Being an SUV, the Countryman aims to provide small families with a multi-functional vehicle that boasts plenty of space as well as fun driving characteristics; it therefore has a longer wheelbase, a much roomier cabin space and higher ground clearance in comparison to the Clubman estate. However, it is important to understand that MINI's ALL4 doesn't make the Countryman an off-road warrior that could live up to the expectations of a Land Rover.

As an option, the Cooper S and Cooper D variants are available with permanent ALL4 all-wheel-drive, an electrohydraulic differential positioned directly on the final drive, varying the distribution from front to rear in an infinite process. ALL4 allows the Countryman to cope better in a range of conditions and when driving on rugged surfaces. In normal driving conditions, up to 50 per cent of the power generated is used to drive the rear wheels, but in extreme conditions this increases to 100 per cent. This drivetrain technology is based on the high-end MINI suspension, including the front axle with MacPherson spring struts and forged track-rod arms, the multi-arm rear axle, and electric power steering with Servotronic.

The Countryman also received dynamic stability control (DSC) as standard, dynamic traction control (DTC) as standard on either the Cooper S or Cooper

ABOVE: **The Countryman was announced in January 2010 as MINI's first Crossover SUV.** NEWSPRESS

LEFT: **The Countryman is offered in a choice of two- or four-wheel-drive (known as ALL4).** NEWSPRESS

D ALL4 models, and an electronic limited-slip differential for the front axle. As far as MINIs go, this was the largest and most unfamiliar variant to leave the production line. Most people would refer to this particular car as a 'biggie', because it is significantly larger than the R56 family and sits higher off the ground. It comes with the standard four-seat arrangement, but is even offered with a three-seat bench at no extra cost, helping to provide more room for larger families.

ALL4 allows the Countryman to cope better on a range of surfaces and driving conditions. NEWSPRESS

The Countryman was designed to provide more room for larger families. NEWSPRESS

THE COUPÉ

MINI first revealed the Coupé in June 2011: it was the first two-seater MINI, and the first to feature a three-box design, where the engine compartment, passenger compartment and luggage compartments are all separated. In John Cooper Works specification, the Coupé also became the fastest production MINI to hit the road, with a 0–100km/h sprint time of 6.4sec and a top speed of 149mph (240km/h). The Coupé could also be ordered with the most powerful petrol and diesel engines in the brand's line-up, leaving buyers with a choice of the 122bhp

Cooper Coupé, the 143bhp Cooper SD Coupé, the 184bhp Cooper S Coupé and the range-topping 208bhp JCW Coupé, all of which are mated to a six-speed manual gearbox.

Built at MINI Plant Oxford, the Coupé shares the same floorpan as the MINI Convertible, ensuring that it has the strongest body of all models. The Coupé's 'helmet roof' was the key talking point for the model variant, which featured a fixed spoiler at the rear of the roof, and an active spoiler that rises from the lower section of the hatch at 50mph (80km/h) and drops down again at 37mph (60km/h), to help improve aerodynamic balance and road grip at high speeds by reducing lift at the rear axle. Since the Coupé doesn't have rear seats, it does boast a healthy-sized boot space at 280ltr (9.9cu ft), making it an ideal and practical vehicle choice for two people. Also adding to its appeal, prices for the MINI Coupé remained similar to the Hatch and Convertible, with prices starting from £16,640 for the Cooper and rising to £23,795 for the JCW.

Following the announcement that the new Coupé would go on sale in October 2011, MINI also revealed details of a racing Coupé – the John Cooper Works Coupé Endurance – specifically developed to compete in the forthcoming twenty-four-hour race at the Nürburgring in June; however, this never reached production. The tweaked 1.6-litre JCW unit could churn out an astonishing 247bhp and up to

239Nm of torque on over-boost. The JCW Coupé is cramped, completely impractical and ludicrously loud, but more importantly, it is a hell of a lot of fun, true MINI style.

THE TWO-MILLIONTH MINI

A decade after the very first R50 MINI rolled off the production line at MINI Plant Oxford, the 2 millionth example was driven off the line by Prime Minister David Cameron in September 2011. Frank-Peter Arndt, responsible for MINI production, was in attendance to celebrate the latest milestone for both MINI and Plant Oxford, which had already seen its fair share of automotive icons fire up into life. Of the 2 million MINIs produced since 2001, more than 1.5 million had been exported from the UK, much like its predecessor, which left BMC and BL struggling to meet home-market demand towards its final days.

The 2-millionth MINI to be built was a Convertible, specially painted in White Silver metallic with a Blue Denim roof. Since this was a very special MINI, it received a range of bespoke interior and exterior qualities, including a distinctive leather steering wheel and lounge leather upholstery. This historic car was also given away as a prize in the global Facebook campaign 'Two Million MINIs – Two Million Faces'. The competition was pretty much what it said on the tin: 2 million photographs of 2 million

ABOVE: **The Coupé was revealed in June 2011, and would become the first two-seater MINI.** NEWSPRESS

ABOVE: **Since the Coupé doesn't have rear seats, it boasts a healthy-sized 280ltr (9.9cu ft) boot.** NEWSPRESS

A decade after the very first R50 MINI rolled off the production line at MINI Plant Oxford, the 2 millionth example was driven off the line by Prime Minister David Cameron in September 2011. NEWSPRESS

MINI fan faces collected to create a dedicated Facebook 'wall'. Of the 2 million participants, one lucky winner was awarded the official 2-millionth MINI. It was during this event that Frank-Peter Arndt briefed David Cameron on BMW Group's preparations to produce the third generation MINI, as well as new production facilities, helping to ensure a bright future for MINI Plant Oxford and thousands of jobs at the pressing plant in Swindon and the engine plant at Hams Hall near Birmingham.

The latest investment into the production facilities also took the company's total investment figures across all UK operations to more than £1.5 billion since the year 2000. To put that in perspective, in 2001 approximately 2,400 associates worked in single shift operations, building 300 cars per day; by 2011 this had grown to 3,700 working a full five days per week to produce 900 MINIs per day. This means that maximum production capacity at Plant Oxford had risen from 100,000 to more than 200,000 units per year.

LONDON OLYMPICS 2012: THE OFFICIAL PARTNER OF TEAM GB AND PARALYMPICS GB

In 2012, the Olympics and Paralympics hit London – another perfect opportunity for MINI to shine. As the official partner of Team GB and Paralympics GB, MINI celebrated the Olympic Games by unveiling the London 2012 special: a limited edition of just 2,012 models, available in Cooper, Cooper D, Cooper S and Cooper SD form. As you'd expect,

MINI celebrated the Olympic Games by unveiling the London 2012 special: a limited edition of just 2,012 models. NEWSPRESS

One of the London 2012 MINI's more striking features is the London skyline, which is stitched across the width of the Piano Black dashboard. NEWSPRESS

THE MINI-ME

MINI's involvement in London 2012 didn't end with the launch of a special edition: the brand was also busy helping out in the Olympic stadium. If MINI wasn't what people would call a 'small car' before, it certainly was now, because the infield of the Olympic Stadium was managed by a team of three MINI-me remote-control cars, helping to support the athletes. The little cars – roughly a quarter scale of the full-sized MINI – had been developed to carry a load of up to 8kg (18lb), two javelins or a singe hammer, discus or shot, and return them back from the field to the throwing areas to help save time during competition. They were powered by batteries that could last for up to 35min during continuous usage, with a radio-control range of 100m (328ft). Designed and built to a strict specification with LOCOG, the cars were all blue and wrapped in the same Olympic Games livery as the full-size fleet of official cars. The equipment could easily be placed and removed from inside the MINI-me's cabin via the open sunroof. Of course, the little cars didn't have a mind of their own and were operated by Game Makers, who'd had a lot of practice in controlling the cars around the infield.

The infield of the Olympic Stadium was managed by a team of three MINI-me remote-control cars. NEWSPRESS

The MINIs did their fair share of exercise, travelling at least 4 miles (6.4km) per day during four-hour shifts across the full nine days of the London 20120 Games. As much as MINI fans would be desperate to get their hands on one, the MINI-mes were never offered to the public and are kept under lock and key at Oxford MINI until their next adventure call. They say good things come in small packages, and in this case, big things came in small packages.

the cars were available in a 'red, white and blue' colour scheme, to honour the British Union Jack: Chilli Red, White Silver or Lightning Blue. To complete the design, each model was also given white mirror caps and a white roof, featuring the London 2012 Olympic graphic.

The London 2012 special was also given a Union Flag sport strip, starting on the bonnet and ending at the boot. As well as bearing the official London Olympic decals, the limited edition can easily be identified by its bespoke grey 17in conical spoke alloy wheels.

However, it is inside the cabin that the MINI 2012 special really comes into its own: one of its more striking features is the London skyline, which has been stitched across the width of the Piano Black dashboard, silhouetting many of the city's most iconic landmarks such as the London Eye, Tower Bridge and Battersea Power Station. To remind passengers that they're driving in a unique little car, the dashboard also reads 'London 1 of 2012'. The 2012 special hit the roads in March 2012, to coincide with the build-up to the London Olympic opening. Thankfully, the prices didn't rocket for this particular edition. By this point, MINI had already positioned itself mid-way between value for money and premium, and understood the importance of remaining accessible, especially on such a monumental occasion. The Cooper hatch had a set price of £17,800, the Cooper D Hatch followed at £19,080, the Cooper S reached £20,125, with the Cooper SD ending at £20,860.

THE MINI ROADSTER

In spring 2012, MINI launched the convertible version of the Coupé, the MINI Roadster, which, like its hardtop sibling, was available across the range: the Cooper, Cooper S, Cooper SD and JCW. The Roadster, which became the sixth member of the MINI family, marked another first for MINI, being the first open-topped two-seater in the brand's history. It was built at Plant Oxford in Cowley, and MINI claimed that the Roadster was the successor to the traditional British roadsters of the past. The Coupé was already tight on space, so taking off the roof wouldn't appeal to buyers who relied on the boot space. However, the semi-automatic soft-top didn't compromise the Roadster's practicality in any way. It still boasts the through-loading, 240ltr (52gal) boot space, and features the same stowage areas behind the two seats. The Roadster models were priced between the entry level Cooper at £18,015 and the range-topping JCW at £24,850.

Like the hardtop Coupé, the Roadster was powered by BMW's latest generation 4-cylinder petrol and diesel units, with power ranging from 122bhp to 211bhp, while mpg fluctuated between 49.6mpg (5.7ltr/100km) and 38.7mpg (7.3ltr/100km) – depending on driving style. The Roadster's moulded A-pillars and windscreen helped to reduce the front area of the car, meaning drag was also reduced. Coupled with the active rear spoiler, this means you can actually feel the Roadster sticking to the tarmac.

In spring 2012, MINI launched the convertible version of the Coupé – the MINI Roadster. NEWSPRESS

All Roadster models also received electric power steering (EPS) with speed-sensitive assistance and Sport mode as standard, allowing the driver to adjust the car's steering characteristics and throttle responses, depending on the road and weather conditions. For customers who opt for a six-speed automatic gearbox, the Sport button also reduces shift times, meaning the Roadster can plough through the gears much more quickly than those with a standard six-speed manual. But just because it was fast, that didn't mean to say it wasn't efficient. The Roadster was also equipped with the brand's MINIMALISM environmental technology as standard, which includes the auto stop/start system, shift point display and brake energy regeneration. In addition, the Roadster featured innovative encapsulation of the drivetrain, which shortens the warm-up period after a cold start and helps to reduce the amount of fuel it gulps during that process.

At launch, the new soft-top two-seater also came with a rather generous range of standard equipment (quite unusual for a MINI), including speed-sensitive steering assistance, heated mirrors, air conditioning, an MP3-compatible CD player and rear parking sensors. Just in case having the top down wasn't enough of a tell-tale giveaway, the Roadster can be identified by its paint finish, in either two non-metallic or six metallic shades with a black roof and sports stripes,

which are available in three colours, and 15in, 16in or 17in alloy wheels – the colour scheme and additional personalized stripes is what differentiates one Roadster from the next.

LONDON-BASED SPECIAL EDITIONS

Since MINI had already let its obsession with London and the 2012 Olympic Games be known, it was no surprise that the brand was planning another two special editions. Looking back, the marque's obsession with London actually began in the 1980s, when Austin Rover launched the Mini Mayfair and the Mini Piccadilly. In March 2012, it was the MINI Baker Street and MINI Bayswater that were preparing to go on sale in 100 global markets, exclusive to the MINI Hatchback. Once again, the special edition cars remained rather modest in appearance, with only fine detailing distinguishing them from the rest.

For the MINI Baker Street and Bayswater, the focus was on colour schemes and trim levels. The Baker Street was available in One, One D, Cooper and Cooper D guise, finished in Rooftop Grey, or optional Pepper White and Midnight Black, with twin black bonnet stripes. The look was completed by 16in, six-star, twin-spoke alloy wheels in high-gloss black, to match the mirror cap, with 'Baker Street'

Following the Olympic Games, MINI launched the Baker Street and Bayswater editions. NEWSPRESS

Like its predecessor, the GP2 was also limited to a 2,000-only production run.
NEWSPRESS

decals added to the side scuttles and door sills. Much like the other MINIs, the Baker Street's standard equipment list included automatic air conditioning, DAB radio, Bluetooth, fog lamps, and a multi-coloured interior lighting package. The entry-level MINI One Baker Street was priced from £16,365, while the top of the range Cooper D Baker Street with an automatic gearbox started from £19,945.

While the Baker Street MINI was a conventional run-around, the Bayswater was labelled the sportier option, available on the MINI variants with more power: the Cooper, Cooper D, Cooper S and Cooper SD. The Bayswater was finished in Kite Blue metallic paint and 17in, high-gloss black, sandblast alloy wheels with machined rim and spoke edges, both of which are bespoke to the model. The Bayswater couldn't be without 'go-faster' sport stripes on the bonnet, which were finished in blue and grey.

Being the sportier of the two cars, the Bayswater came with a larger price tag. The base model Cooper Bayswater started from £18,565, while the Cooper SD Bayswater with an automatic gearbox started from £23,375. Both cars came with a six-speed manual gearbox as standard, with an automatic transmission available as an option. The brand's MINIMALISM technology also lowered the CO_2 emissions of the One D and Cooper D models to 99g/km, making the two cars exempt from the London congestion charge – an added bonus for MINI fans living in and around the city.

THE GP2

Six years after the original Mini JCW Kit (GP1) stole our hearts away, BMW took the GP specification to another level. Since the all-new, second generation MINI had gone on sale in 2007, it was about time the GP was revived in the car's new form. Sticking to the same raw, two-seater formula, the new GP – labelled GP2 – could clearly be distinguished through its beefed-up body kit and chintzy additions – only now, in 2012, the car was pushing £29,000, a price that wouldn't just leave your pocket empty, but with a gaping great hole in it. Like its predecessor, the GP2 was also limited to a 2,000-only production run. The one significant difference between the two cars was the switch from a supercharger to a turbocharger, since all second generation MINI Cooper S and JCW variants received a 1.6-litre turbo engine over the former supercharged unit. Somehow, the turbo never lived up to the charm of whining supercharger (which also helped to disguise the less attractive whine from the failing power-steering pump), and the loss of the mechanical diff meant that it didn't feel as planted on the road, either.

THE GROUNDBREAKING MINI: THE PACEMAN

Since the Countryman hadn't turned out to be a huge hit with all MINI customers – or any good at

The Paceman became the seventh model of the MINI family, hitting the road in 2013. NEWSPRESS

gaining new ones, for that matter – BMW set out to broaden MINI's target market by launching a cross between the MINI hatch and the MINI Countryman. This car would be named the Paceman, a three-door SAV (sports activity coupé). Following the car's appearance as a concept car at the Detroit Motor Show in 2011, senior vice-president of MINI brand management, Dr Kay Segler, announced in 2012 that

'the MINI Paceman is the official name of the brand's seventh model', and would go on sale in 2013 with an entry-level starting price of £18,970.

Introduced to celebrate ten years since the re-launch of the Mini marque, the Countryman Coupé – and the seventh MINI addition to the MINI range – would be built at Magna Steyr in Austria, alongside its bigger brother. Essentially, the Paceman was designed

The Paceman marked the beginning of a new design language, ahead of the third generation MINI. NEWSPRESS

to appeal to customers who desired a spacious four-wheel-drive, but in the form of a coupé rather than a five-door saloon. The coupé interpretation of the Countryman is available in four versions, including the MINI Cooper S, which has an impressive 0–100km/h time of just 7.3sec – a rather impressive figure for a bulky MINI. Although the Coupé looked smaller than the Countryman, looks can be very deceiving, and bumper-to-bumper the Paceman Cooper was almost identical to the Countryman in length, at 4,109mm. This extended to 4,115mm for the Cooper S and Cooper SD Paceman models.

The Paceman also marked the beginning of a new design language, ahead of the third generation MINI. Its hexagonal grille and chrome surround gave it an immediate presence, not to mention its long, raked doors with blacked-out pillars, designed to create a 'floating roof' effect, similar to that of the MINI Coupé. To personalize the Paceman, the roof can be finished in black, white or body colour (not MINI's most exciting colour theme), and slopes towards the rear of the car with an integrated spoiler. The horizontal rear lights curve from the rear to the side of the car, and it is these that were a first for the MINI. Since the Paceman was a rather different-looking MINI, it became the first model in the line-up to feature a rear nameplate. This would also become a standard feature for the Countryman later in the year, since it became apparent that the two cars were so similar in appearance that it was difficult for everyone to tell the difference.

The Paceman was also responsible for another MINI first, thanks to its innovative rear seat arrangement, which had been styled around a lounge concept and was strictly a two-seater. The arrangement provides such a level of increased head and legroom that, as a passenger, you actually feel as though you are sat in a lounge chair, especially with the integrated armrests and seat support. Although the Paceman is strictly a four-seater car, it is still practical. Focusing on the rear of the car, folding down the rear seats expands the boot space from 330 to 1,080ltr (11.7 to 38.1cu ft), which is easily accessed through the high-opening tailgate.

Although the Paceman features the signature centre speedometer, bespoke to MINI, another new addition to the MINI design was a black surround and decorative inner rings in high-gloss black or chrome. Similarly the window controls, which on every MINI up to this point had been in the form of toggle switches sat below the speedo, were moved to the trim panel on the doors, like the majority of cars on the road.

From launch the Paceman was offered with the choice of two petrol and two diesel engines, all of which were mated to a six-speed manual gearbox, or the optional automatic with Steptronic function for manual control. The 1.6-litre, 122bhp petrol unit offers a 0–60mph time of 10.4sec with a combined fuel consumption of 47.1mpg (6ltr/100km). The higher-performance Cooper S uses the same engine but is turbocharged and tuned to deliver 184bhp: this means it will sprint to 62mph (100km/h) in 7.5sec. The Cooper D uses a 1.6-litre 112bhp turbocharged engine, which can reach 0–60mph in an impressive 10.8sec, as well as providing 64.2mpg (4.4ltr/100km). The Cooper SD gained a 2.0-litre, 143bhp unit, with a 0–60mph time of 9.2sec and a consumption figure of 61.4mpg (4.6ltr/100km).

Like the Countryman, the Paceman Cooper D, Cooper SD and Cooper S were also available with MINI's ALL4 four-wheel-drive system. Benefiting from MINI's highly praised chassis technology, comprising MacPherson spring struts and forged cross members on the front axle, a multi-link rear axle and electric power steering with Servotronic, the Paceman is satisfyingly agile in the corners. Like the Countryman, the Paceman is also fitted with a range of driver aids, including dynamic stability control (DSC) standard across the range, and gadgets such as dynamic traction control (DTC) and electronic differential lock control (EDLC) available on the Cooper S, Cooper SD and Cooper D ALL4 models. The Paceman is the sensible car for not-so-sensible customers.

The Paceman didn't stay sensible for long, though. In December 2012, MINI unveiled the JCW version of the sensible SAV, which eventually hit the roads in March 2013. It could reach a top speed of 140mph (225km/h), and its hefty horsepower was achieved through using the same engine that powered the Countryman JCW – the 1.6-litre, 215bhp with MINI ALL4. This particular model played a key role in pushing MINI prices even further, becoming the first MINI to achieve £30,000. Fitted with the six-speed CVT

Steptronic automatic gearbox or the standard six-speed manual, the JCW Paceman could hit 62mph (100km/h) in under 7sec, and with manual transmission, had an estimated combined fuel consumption figure of 38.2mpg (7.4ltr/100km). The key alterations were made under the Paceman's shell, where the suspension has been lowered by 10mm and the stability control system received an additional DTC mode, where the ALL4 torque split can be altered to send the full 100 per cent of its power to the rear wheels, rather than a 50/50 split.

In terms of appearance, the JCW Paceman can't be missed, sharing the same red and black colour scheme – inside and out – as the outgoing MINI JCW models. The Chilli Red shade is reserved for the John Cooper Works model, and is stitched into the lounge leather sports seats, the sports steering wheel and the gear gaiter. The JCW Paceman features the same bold and seductive features as the MINI GP, with its twin viper stripes running along the length of the car, and its prominent aerodynamic kit.

MINI GOES COMMERCIAL: THE MINI CLUBVAN

Looking at the MINI range, it would appear that one particular model had been overlooked. Since Austin and Morris had released the Mini Pick-Up and Mini Van in the mid-1960s, it only seemed right that the modern MINI should follow in the same footsteps: enter the MINI Clubvan. It made its global debut at the Goodwood Festival of Speed in 2012, and was labelled a premium commercial vehicle with greater looks than the over-traditional work-horses. Based on the foundations of the MINI Clubman, the Clubvan was built at Plant Oxford in Cowley; featuring the same powertrain and chassis technology, it has five doors with split rears and a 'Clubdoor'.

The Clubvan was launched in three forms: a MINI One Clubvan with 98bhp, the Cooper Clubvan with 122bhp and the Cooper D with 112bhp; all of them came with MINI's front-wheel-drive set-up with electric power steering, MacPherson front suspension and multi-link rear suspension, and a six-speed manual gearbox as standard, although the six-speed automatic was also available. The boot space occupied the entire rear space, extending back from the rear double doors to the internal bulkhead – made from solid aluminium with a steel mesh – behind the driver and passenger seats.

The body-coloured side panels, where the Clubman's windows would usually sit, featured polycarbonate reinforcement and provided the perfect canvas for business owners to display their brand name. The Clubvan does mean MINI, too, as not only does it boast a 115cm (45in) load area, which is also more than 102cm (40in) wide, it can also be loaded to the roofline, which is 84cm (33in) at its highest point. In total, the Clubvan has an 860ltr (30.4cu ft) luggage space. Unlike the Clubman, the commercial MINI was notably cheaper than the other seven members of the MINI family. Starting with the bottom-of-the-range One Clubvan, prices started from £11,175 and rose to £13,600 for the Cooper D.

The Clubvan made its global debut at the Goodwood Festival of Speed in 2012. NEWSPRESS

CHAPTER NINE

THE BUYER'S GUIDE

Speaking from experience, owning a MINI will prompt you to feel a number of emotions, usually in one go. A MINI has the ability to make you feel enormously frustrated and immensely satisfied in equal measures. It has been perfectly packaged to create the world's class-leading modern-day hatchback, but that doesn't mean it's innocent of causing a few hiccups, here and there. While the modern MINI is an absolute pleasure to drive and is sure to get you cracking a smile on the open road at the peak of summer, any MINI enthusiast will know that the first generation R50 MINI suffered from two very distinctive failures: the weak Rover Midland five-speed gearbox and the noisy power-steering pump.

A TEMPERAMENTAL MIDLAND GEARBOX

As mentioned a little earlier, Mk1 R50 MINI Ones and Coopers, built between 2001 and 2004, did, and still can, suffer from fatal gearbox failure, in fact so much so that the Midland gearbox is one of the most common gearboxes found in workshops. To paint a picture, the Midland box was pieced together using bearings that later proved to be rather weak. The two in question are the front and pinion bearings on the lay gear, found on either side of the crown wheel on the diff. By this point, as the driver, you would usually notice a distinctive whining noise, accompanied by gear crunches and grinds. You may even find yourself stuck in gear, or suffering a slipping clutch or loss of power. When the bearings eventually collapse, the crown wheel is no longer supported and will freely grind a hole through the bell housing.

In extreme cases, workshops have seen gear sets chewed and gearbox casings cracked – costly damage that is deemed non-repairable, the only option being to buy a new gearbox. What is more, if you do find yourself with a broken gearbox, you'll likely need a new clutch too, due to oil contamination.

Today, dealers only fit reconditioned gearboxes to R50 MINI Ones and Coopers, since it is well known within the industry and MINI circles that the Midland box is nothing short of a disaster waiting to happen. Drivers can even choose to convert their MINIs to accommodate the later, more fined Getrag gearbox of 2004 – but that involves changing other parts to match the new set-up, including the driveshafts, gearbox

The Midland box was pieced together using bearings that later proved to be weak.

Drivers can choose to convert their MINIs to have the later, more refined Getrag gearbox of 2004.

mounting, gear linkage cables, slave cylinder, clutch and flywheel. This also rings true for the more adventurous owners who wish to drop the six-speed Getrag gearbox from the Cooper S and John Cooper Works models into their modest Ones and Coopers.

Luckily, the performance models such as the Cooper S were fitted with a stronger, more advanced six-speed Getrag gearbox from production, so did not suffer from grinding gears. And thankfully for owners, replacing the gearbox isn't too much of an issue – in fact, for keen MINI enthusiasts and mechanics, it's easy enough to drop the old one out and fit a new one yourself. The beauty of the R50 MINI, and all models leading up to the second generation model of 2006, is that it was almost as accessible as the classic Mini we all adored working on. Knowing that you can lift the bonnet in the comfort of your own driveway on a warm Saturday morning and get to work on repairing your little car with your own hands, makes owning a MINI even more joyous. It is cheaper, too, since you only need worry about paying for parts, and not the hefty bills that tend to come with hourly rates for garage repairs.

A NOISY POWER-STEERING PUMP

The MINI features a different type of power-steering set-up to most other cars on the road today. Rather than being driven by the engine belts, the power-steering pump is driven by an electric motor, which means that the pump is always at risk of getting hot. It doesn't help that the pump is also located directly below the exhaust manifold, placing it in a predominantly high temperature environment. Unlike the gearbox hiccups, the power-steering issue isn't quite as vigorous, and usually the driver will only ever complain of a constant whining from under the bonnet. Most of the time this is due to how the pump is powered, and it doesn't necessarily mean that it will fail. If it does, the worst problem you'll face is a heavy steering wheel, which, if you owned a classic Mini, will be rather familiar to you – build up those arm muscles.

Replacing the power-steering pump is another 'do it yourself' job, if you prefer to work on your own cars. First, disconnect the battery in order to cut power to the starter motor, then remove the cap on the power-steering fluid reservoir. You need to remove as much of the fluid as possible – a task that can be made slightly easier by using kitchen utensils such as a turkey baster to suck up the excess fluid – to prevent it from pouring all over your work area. The next step is to detach the reservoir from the mounting bracket on the firewall, to give you some slack on the fluid lines.

You then need to slide underneath the MINI to unbolt the power-steering fan from the pump bracket: this is only held on by two 13mm nuts. With the

MINI EXPERIENCES

PENELOPE STOTHERT – A MINI FOR ALL AGES

My first encounter with a MINI was when I purchased my 2005-reg Cooper in Silver. Due to my career, I was usually equipped with a company car, which was upgraded on a regular basis. I never really needed to think about the buying and ownership process, or what I'd look for in a car if I were to purchase one privately. In any case, my company cars were usually the feisty sorts, ranging from powerful BMWs to luxurious Mercedes – I've always been a BMW girl, having owned my fair share of M cars during my younger years.

However, when it came to retirement, I did need to start looking for a car. Having gone round in circles, I ended up back where I started: with an iconic small car. I had had a classic Mini when I was a teenager, and I'd ended up with the modern-day version: BMW's MINI Cooper. I'd gone back to my youth. It was a brilliant car to drive, and I had some fun with it – I

even took it to 'Mini in the Park' at Santa Pod. One thing that the little MINI did feature as an optional extra was the sports suspension, though as you become more mature you become a little weary of it.

I had my Cooper for more than five years before I started looking for something a little more sensible earlier this year. I did look at getting a VW Golf, but they don't seem to boast any personality. So, if you hadn't guessed, I ended up getting another little MINI. I had no intention of purchasing a Cooper S, though had my eye on one at our local garage. But once I had taken it for a test drive, I knew I had to buy it. There's something about a MINI that you just can't help but fall in love with. Unlike the Cooper I had owned, the quality of the suspension has changed and the car as a whole feels much more premium: it's like sitting in a BMW again, because it oozes quality.

Penelope believes the MINI is the 'most stylish hatchback on the market'.

(continued overleaf)

PENELOPE STOTHERT – A MINI FOR ALL AGES

My Cooper is finished in Eclipse Grey and features the Chilli Pack with a few extra nuts and bolts, including Sports Mode, which tightens the wheel; I love feeling what the car is doing through the steering as it gives you more confidence on the road. I really like the turbo on the Cooper S: it makes a great noise, and the car itself holds the road really well. If I were to be a bit picky, I'd say that the second generation MINI doesn't look very nice at the back, like the Mk1 does. But I am impressed with the attention to detail inside the cabin, such as the ambient lights in the door panels and in the footwell. Having owned an original Mini, I've always been impressed by BMWs new creation, and I have to say, in my opinion, it's the most stylish hatchback on the market. I think the MINI is an accessible car for all ages, and creates a unique social image. I love it.

MINI EXPERIENCES

LUCY FINLAY

I had never been too fussed about driving a MINI; I could appreciate them for what they were but it had never been something I was desperate to do. It wasn't until I started my new job at BMW that things began to change.

Of course, working in a BMW garage meant that we had a MINI centre next door to the business. I'd seen them coming in, usually in the popular pepper white colour, but there would often be the typical pretty girl driving, I guess for the status factor, so that automatically put me off straight away. I'm not the kind of girl who appreciates a car for being 'cute' or 'pretty'; plus, by this time I had driven pretty much every BMW in the range, so I was sure that I was destined to own one of those.

It all changed one day though, when I came out of the dealership to move a bunch of trade cars to the other site. I got thrown the keys to a MINI. Not just any MINI, but the MINI that would become my own prized possession. As I held the key in my hand, I walked up to the car while clicking the unlock button, waiting to see a 'girly' car with hideous stick-on eyelashes, flash at me. But to my surprise, I had come face-to-face with something much different to what I had imagined.

The MINI in question was a 2011-plate Cooper SD. It was Laser Blue with a black roof and spoiler, as well as black bonnet stripes, 17-inch silver alloy wheels and, of course, the Xenon headlights. Now, I understand this doesn't sound particularly 'wow', especially when you're used to seeing the premium BMWs driving around, but for a change, this was the kind of MINI I could really appreciate. I jumped in thinking to myself, 'This is great; part leather seats, a line-black roof and push start/stop technology.'

Again, I had come to expect this premium finish in a car, but once I

Lucy fell in love with the MINI as soon as she stepped behind the wheel.

fan out of the way, you can then work on moving the electrical connectors from the pump, followed by the two fluid hose connections – this isn't the easiest job, since the pump is situated in a rather tight spot and lighting will be minimal.

Once you've removed the pump from the subframe, transfer the mounting frame from the old one to the new one. Now you can bolt the new pump to the subframe. Once it's bolted up, reconnect both the electrical and fluid lines, and re-install the fan.

The last job is to refill the pump reservoir, and ensure you bleed it. BMW MINI specifies that only the product CHF-11S should be used, as it is specially formulated for use in electric power-steering pumps: the fluid is much thinner than regular power-steering fluids you're likely to find on the shelf, and prevents the pump from overworking itself. Once you've filled the reservoir to the MAX mark, start the engine and proceed to turn the steering wheel on full lock left to right, in order to help bleed the air from the system. During this procedure, keep an eye on the fluid level, as it may require a top-up.

So there you go: another relatively simple repair that can be carried out at home.

had sat inside the MINI, I felt that I was in a high-end car and not something flimsy. I didn't quite expect this quality from a MINI. As you can probably tell, I was rapidly falling in love with this car, but it's the next part of this story that really persuaded me to seal the deal. I pushed the key in and pressed the start button.

For a diesel, it was surprisingly quiet and refined. The drive to the other site was about 5½ miles away so I had just enough time to familiarize myself with the car. From the moment that I pushed the accelerator down and felt the power that this little car could produce – in my eyes, it was something close to sheer brilliance – I fell in love. We swept around corners a little 'enthusiastically' and the little car cornered like it was on rails. For a front-wheel-drive car, this was amazing (and not what I was used to) – this MINI could hold the road!

I am not shy when it comes to driving a fast car but as soon as I felt the way this MINI drove, I couldn't stop smiling. When I got out and parked up, my colleague walked up to me and said I was driving it like I had stolen it. It was at this point that I realized I had found my new car – I loved it so much that after my shift I went in and spoke to my manager to see if he would do me a deal on it. After a little negotiation, the deal was done.

It's funny how the car, which I never thought I would ever want, became my favourite car I have ever owned. And once you own a MINI there really is no going back. You also become part of this secret order

among other MINI drivers that people without MINIs don't tend to understand. It's not just a car; they have personality, presence and such a big character for a little car. The more you get to know about them, the more impressed you become with them.

My car has a 2.0-litre turbo diesel engine with 141bhp. Now, compared with what I drove about at work on a daily basis, that probably doesn't sound too impressive. But I can assure you that, for a car as light as mine, it can certainly give some of the big saloons a run for their money – especially at the traffic lights! And that's when you start looking into the history of the brand – those little Minis of old won rally races all over the world, including the Monte Carlo Rally. You get a sense of pride in owning a MINI and you remember that you're driving a car inspired by the classic that people like Mick Jagger and Lulu once owned.

I know the new BMW MINI is based on German engineering. However, they still come to life at Plant Oxford and I firmly believe that there is not one person who can jump into a MINI and not get out without a huge smile on their face. One of the funniest things that I learned when I went on the many courses I was sent on with BMW was that 80 per cent of people who own a MINI will name it. I was, and still am, one of those people. By this point, I had named all of my cars and, from the start, it seemed like Bert and I were destined to be together.

CHAPTER TEN

THE THIRD GENERATION MINI: A NEW BEGINNING WITH F56

In November 2013, after 1,041,412 examples had been built, the very last R56 MINI rolled off the production line at Plant Oxford. Since the launch of the modern MINI in 2001, more than 2.4 million models had been produced by the dedicated engineers at Cowley, and in the space of ten years, MINI had evolved into a second generation car, had seen the introduction of turbochargers from superchargers for the Cooper S and JCW 4-cylinder MINI variants, and welcomed MINIMALISM technologies for improved fuel economy and performance. As well as that, MINI also accounted for 14 per cent of all UK vehicle exports in 2012, confirming its position as one of the leading marques in the automotive industry. But this wasn't a sad occasion, it was very much a joyous one, because production of the all-new F56

MINI was already underway at Cowley, marking a new era for the MINI brand.

In 2013 BMW MINI unveiled the next generation model of its iconic hatchback, when the German-owned manufacturer took its dividing design to yet another level. The launch of the next generation MINI – codenamed F56 – was officially made at MINI Plant Oxford on 18 November – the day that Sir Alec Issigonis would have turned 107. Although it still features a number of unmistakable brand characteristics, the original BMW model has undergone a full redesign. The exterior has been noticeably reshaped, with both the front and rear end benefiting from prominent facelifts, while the interior now boasts a number of technical upgrades. At the launch of the new F56 MINI at Plant Oxford, Andres

The MINI family had become the most beloved hatchback across the world.
NEWSPRESS

BMW MINI F56 Cooper 1.5 3dr (2015)

Layout and chassis
Three-door, four-seat hatchback with steel body
Chassis: Steel UKL platform
Transmission: M6
Engine Platform: B38A15MO

No. of doors: 3
No. of seats: 4

Engine
Type: 1.5-litre, in-line
No. of cylinders: 3
Valves: 12
No. of valves per cylinder: 4
Compression ratio: 11:1
Displacement: 1499cc
Stroke/Bore: 94.6/82mm
Power output: 134bhp
Max. torque: 220Nm
Engine control: MEVD 17.2.3
Charging type: TwinPower Turbo
Injection type: High precision direct injection

Transmission
Type: 6MTT220
1st 3.615
2nd 1.952
3rd 1.241
4th 0.969
5th 0.806
6th 0.683

Suspension and steering
Suspension front: MacPherson Struts, adjustable
    dampers, anti-roll bar
Suspension rear: Multi-link, anti-roll bar

Steering type: Rack and pinion
Steering ratio: 14.2:1

Tyres
Tyre size front: 175/65 R15 84 H
Tyre size rear: 175/65 R15 84 H

Wheel size front: 5.5 J × 15 alloys
Wheel size rear: 5.5 J × 15 alloys

Brakes
Brake front: Ventilated discs
Brake rear: Solid discs

Dimensions
Vehicle length: 3,821mm (150in)
Vehicle width: 1,727mm (68in)
Vehicle height: 1,414mm (56in)
Wheelbase: 2,495mm (98in)
Turning circle: 10.8m (35ft)
Overhang front: 749mm (29in)
Overhang rear: 577mm (23in)
Track front: 1,501mm (59in)
Track rear: 1,501mm (59in)
Luggage capacity: 211–731 litres (7.5–25.8cu ft)
Tank capacity: 40 litres (8.8gal)

Curb weight: 1,085/1,160kg (2,392/2,558lb)
Axle load ratio, rear: 37.9 per cent
Gross vehicle weight: 1,565kg (3,451lb)
Payload: 480kg (1,058lb)
Axle load limit front: 870kg (1,918lb)
Axle load limit rear: 755kg (1,665lb)

Performance
Top speed: 130mph (209km/h)
Acceleration 0–60mph: 7.9 seconds

Fuel consumption
Combined: 62.8mpg (4.5ltr/100km)
CO_2 emissions: 105g/km

Warming, head of design at MINI UK, said: 'This has possibly been the most emotional and rewarding MINI we've built yet. Achieving the right balance of heritage and innovation has been a significant part in producing the next generation Mini hatchback.'

Warming explained that while the new MINI is a completely new car, the design team worked to build on the standard symbolic features, while introducing distinctive heritage elements we have yet to see on a modern MINI: 'While the MINI is a completely new car, we've enhanced the existing elements to ensure the car remains 100 per cent MINI – so it resembles the classic Mini more than its predecessor. The new, larger grille is a perfect example of this – it's clearly a MINI, but it is completely brand new.'

In fact the new MINI is visually different from every angle – the side panels now consist of curved lines, while the rear has also been given a full facelift to couple its new distinctive vertical (and framed) tail lights, which originate from the newest family member, the MINI Paceman. As Warming says: 'The door handles and wing mirrors are still the same, but we've made them more accessible. The car has been lengthened slightly, it features significant curves and crease lines which give a sense of speed whilst standing still, and inside we have enabled driver interaction with the improved infotainment screen.'

One change that was bound to come as a shock to MINI drivers is that the speedo is no longer located centrally in the next generation's interior, but has instead been positioned alongside the rev counter to form a cluster in front of the driver. Warming said of this: 'The speedo, which is such a unique feature to MINI, has moved directly opposite the driver. Unlike before, the infotainment screen now enables driver interaction by displaying a number of visual features from a virtual rev counter to highlighting changes in drive modes or displaying the control of the in-car temperature gauge.'

It's not just the styling elements that have been given a makeover: the new MINI Hatch also comes with the option of three brand new, TwinPower Turbo Technology Valvetronic petrol engines. Upgrading from the 1.6-litre unit, the 2014 range was powered by more powerful 3- and 4-cylinder engines. The Cooper and Cooper D downsized to more efficient 1.5-litre 3-cylinder petrol and diesel engines, while the powerful Cooper S runs a larger 2.0-litre 4-cylinder unit, which can produce up to 192bhp.

Chris Brownridge, brand director of MINI UK said: 'The next generation MINI is a completely new car. It features more efficient and more powerful drivetrains, and the in-car equipment Mini is offering in this segment is what you'd usually find in luxury premium cars. Every MINI has to be fun to drive and exciting to own, and the next generation model really reflects these values of ownership experience.'

The new generation MINI hit the road in 2014, with prices starting from £15,300 for the Cooper, £16,450 for the Cooper D, and £18,650 for the Cooper S.

MINI unveiled the next generation model of its iconic hatchback – F56 – on 18 November 2013, the day that Sir Alec Issigonis would have turned 107. NEWSPRESS

PART IV
Mini AND MINI
IN MOTORSPORT

CHAPTER ELEVEN

THE MONTE MINI

The term 'Mini in motor sport' has become something of a traditional chant, not only in the UK but worldwide. The Mini has been labelled a rally legend, since the badge has continued to compete successfully in motor sport over the past five decades, with its first appearance dating back to as early as 1962. Looking back through the history and archives of motor racing, pinpointing exactly where it all began can be quite tricky. But what we do know is that it all started with John Cooper's Mini Cooper. After the birth of the Mini in 1959, Sir Alec Issigonis collaborated with John Cooper – owner of the Cooper Car Company, and the designer and builder of Formula One and rally cars – to build a new addition to the Mini family, after he saw potential in the little car for competition. Issigonis was at first reluctant to see the Mini take the role of a performance car, but after John Cooper appealed to BMC management, the Austin Cooper and Morris Cooper models were soon born and made their debuts in 1961; they were destined to be the sportier, more powerful version of the original Austin.

The 848cc engine from the Morris Mini Minor was given some serious improvements and a full re-build. It was given a longer stroke to increase capacity to 997cc, increasing its power output from just 34bhp to 55bhp. The car featured a racing-tuned engine, twin SU carburettors, a closer-ratio gearbox and front disc brakes, uncommon at the time in a small car. One thousand units of this version were commissioned by BMC, intended for and designed to meet the rules of Group 2 rally racing. In 1964 the 997cc engine was replaced by a shorter stroke 998cc unit.

In 1962 Rhodesian John Love became the first non-British racing driver to win the British Saloon Car Championship driving a Mini Cooper. Developed alongside the Cooper was the further tuned 'S' model, which was later released in 1963. This particular Cooper S remained in production until the model was updated in 1964. Not surprisingly, John Cooper produced two S models specifically for track and circuit racing.

Today, the beloved and equally controversial BMW MINI has become something of a similar icon. In July 2010, the manufacturer announced its plans to enter the World Rally Championship, which thousands of enthusiasts across the globe were ecstatic to hear. Since its birth in the year 2000, the new MINI has become prominent in a number of motor-sport series. Having been filtered down through the generations, the motor-sport DNA of the MINI's predecessor now flows through the veins of the new model. From the MINI Challenge all the way up through the rankings to the international World Rally Championship, the historic marque continues to compete.

The sporty and innovative qualities that saw the Mini Cooper and S drive to victory in the 1960s and 1970s, remain the basic ingredients of the MINI today. With its compact exterior dimensions, the new MINI can simply whisk around corners, resting solidly on its wide track and long wheelbase. Rauno Aaltonen, the 'Flying Finn', is reported to have said: 'Both generations of the Mini clearly stand out from all other cars in precisely the same way. They are extremely agile and follow the steering immediately. Back then the Mini was a princess, beautiful and full of character. In the meantime the princess has grown up, and the new MINI has become a queen.'

The Mini Cooper S took victory in the glorious Monte Carlo Rally three times, in the years 1964,

THE RALLY LEGEND

The Mini Cooper was launched on 20 September 1961, and went on to become one of the world's biggest performance car icons for the next fifty years. The 1960s were essentially the decade of the Mini. Even when the Mini was dominating rally events and starting to pose intense competition on closed circuits, there was still no other car available on the market able to offer the same sporting performance for so little money. The Mini accumulated countless rally wins, the most prestigious of which were achieved in Monte Carlo, where the Mini Cooper won the famous rally three times. Irish rally driver Paddy Hopkirk is the man who put the Mini on the map and the driver who saw the one-off British small car become a motor-sport legend. On 21 January 1964, Paddy Hopkirk and co-driver Henry Liddon drove the Mini Cooper S to victory in the Monte Carlo Rally for the very first time. Paddy Hopkirk's Finnish teammates Timo Makinen and Rauno Aaltonen secured another two overall victories in 1965 and 1967.

The Cooper S was also victorious in the 1966 event, though this has been labelled the most controversial in the history of the Monte Carlo Rally. The top finishers included the three Mini Coopers of Timo Makinen, Rauno Aaltonen and Paddy Hopkirk, with Roger Clark's Ford Cortina in fourth. However, these cars were excluded for having iodine vapour, single filament bulbs in their standard headlights, instead of double-filament dipping bulbs. A further six cars were also disqualified, damaging the credibility of the event; covering the rally, *Motorsport* magazine ran the headline 'The Monte Carlo Fiasco'.

1965 and 1967. Minis proved to be the perfect competitors' car when it came to carrying speed through the corners, and their small build, coupled with their light structure, meant they could be easily manoeuvred and could dart freely between the traffic on a race circuit, giving them a large advantage over other cars on the tarmac, gravel or icy rally track.

The Monte Carlo Rally has been regarded as the toughest event on the rallying circuit ever since its inception in 1911. The rally of 1964 was a particularly memorable one: with Sir Paddy Hopkirk at the wheel alongside co-driver Henry Liddon, the No. 37 Mini Cooper S powered to victory, to the sheer astonishment of the rest of the field. Of course, this victory

Hopkirk and Liddon claimed the winner's trophy at the Monte Carlo Rally in 1964.
NEWSPRESS

was repeated a further two times in the years 1965 and 1967, when the following year the Mini rage had clearly latched on, with a sturdy six Mini Cooper Ss starting on the grid. This time, Timo Makinen and Paul Easter took the chequered flag and outright title,

The 1964 victory was repeated a further two times in the years 1965 and 1967. MAGIC CAR PICS

with Hopkirk and Liddon in twenty-sixth, while Don and Erle Morley finished in twenty-seventh position.

In 1966, Rauno Aaltonen and Liddon crossed the finishing line first, making it a hat-trick of Mini victories. But unfortunately the winning strike turned sour. It is well known throughout history that the Mini rally cars took first, second and third place in the 1966 event, only for all three cars to be disqualified for breaching headlamp regulations, alongside a number of other teams competing in the rally. Ultimately, this caused one of the most controversial arguments in motor sport, when the cars were said to have used a variable resistance headlamp dimming circuit to replace the dual-filament lamps, and were stripped of any title or victory.

Following Mini's first victory in the Monte Carlo Rally, the automotive industry went wild in producing 'go faster' kits and accessories to spec the little car. Ranging from the legendary Downton Engineering Works firm to backstreet tuning fanatics, everyone was out to squeeze as much power as possible from the Mini, even the owners of the modest 848cc cars. It didn't matter that the little car was miniscule and that, in reality, the Mini was deemed a 'sensible' car: everyone who stepped behind the wheel immediately felt like a racing driver, low to the tarmac and a god in the bends.

A DRIVE DOWN VICTORY LANE

The year 1964 was arguably one of the most memorable for the Mini. It was the year that the little car left its mark on the world of motor sport, or specifically, the world of rallying. Irish rally driver Paddy Hopkirk, alongside co-driver Henry Liddon, drove the Mini to the victory lane, after winning the famous Monte Carlo Rally in a Mini Cooper S (1071S), registration number 33EJB. One of the most challenging motor-sport events in the world had been won by a small, low-budget family car. At this stage the public were questioning whether or not there was anything the

small family car couldn't do. To the UK population, the Mini wasn't just a legend: it was now a hero, too. When the victorious car returned from the rally in 1964, it was awarded a triumphant welcome home by the media.

Following the result, and according to AR Online, Issigonis said: 'The amazing point is that I planned the ADO15 not as a competition car, but as family transport. But I think that when exceptional drivers get hold of the car, they can exploit its steering, suspension and road-holding, all of which I felt were important for a family car.'

Irish rally driver Paddy Hopkirk, alongside co-driver Henry Liddon, won the famous Monte Carlo Rally in a Mini Cooper S (107IS) 33EJB.
MAGIC CAR PICS

DOWNTON ENGINEERING WORKS LTD: A BRIEF HISTORY

Known as the ultimate specialist in re-engineering Mini Coopers, Downton Engineering Works was originally formed at the end of the nineteenth century as an agricultural engineering business in the ancient Wiltshire town of Downton, near Salisbury. It was soon developed into a small local motor garage, and was bought by Daniel and Veronica (also known as 'Bunty') Richmond in 1947, where they served the needs of local car owners. The couple clearly had a strong passion for cars, and it wasn't long before they were attracting a new client base: soon Bentleys, Lagondas, Rolls-Royces and Bugattis were coming in for engineering services. Daniel himself was a keen participant in local motor-sport events, as was 'Bunty', competing at hill climb and sprint events in a range of high-octane vehicles. 'Bunty' was also admired for how much she adored her Ferrari 250BGTO.

In the 1950s, the family-owned Downton garage began producing parts and kits to improve the performance of everyday cars, and developed a soft spot for BMC's A-Series engine, particularly when it featured in the new Austin Se7en Mini. The couple's tuning kits were so good that they could increase the horsepower even of a Cooper. The couple adored the Mini so much that they purchased and tuned their very own 1969 Mini, registration plate UHR850; after enjoying a life of racing, this car is now on display at the Heritage Motor Centre at Gaydon.

In the early 1960s, Coopers running with modified Downton cylinder heads and a variety of other tuning components had the edge at competition events. For this reason, the firm was offered a consultancy contract with BMC: the company soon expanded, and BMC's Competitions Department recorded win after win in the early 1960s. Even celebrities were taking their Mini to Daniel and 'Bunty' for conversion. But this point in time would turn out to be the pinnacle of the company's lifetime, and the 1970s were tough for the business, especially as it lost its contract with BMC after the formation of British Leyland. Also, since its employees were leaving and the business was rapidly declining, the couple gradually began to lose interest. Sadly, Daniel died in 1974 and 'Bunty' couldn't tolerate life without him, which eventually led to her tragic suicide two years later; this meant doors had to close on the family-owned business.

But that wasn't the end, although the future did look bleak. Downton Engineering Works was relaunched in the early 1990s under new ownership, and continued to offer tuning products to thousands of Mini enthusiasts and other cars alike, as well as bespoke customer chassis conversions. It eventually went on to build a number of limited-edition Minis during the last days of Rover Mini production.

CHAPTER TWELVE

MINI JOINS THE WORLD RALLY CHAMPIONSHIP

The FIA World Rally Championship has been labelled as one of the toughest motor-sport competitions in the world, ever since its formation in the early 1970s. It hosts thirteen events in thirteen different countries over four continents every year, pushing the drivers, the teams and of course the cars themselves to the very limit. Like most forms of motor sport, the WRC is broadcast on international television, so many people are aware of the variety of surfaces the cars compete on at each venue. From ice and snow to tarmac and dirt tracks, all of which are made even more challenging in the event of heavy rain, scorching sunshine or roads littered with rocks and other objects, it is no wonder the championship has been dubbed one of the most challenging events in history.

For many motor-sport enthusiasts, the arrival of the new BMW MINI brand at the championship was a symbolic and monumental occasion, because it marked the return of the victorious name to the sport after the courageous Cooper S took three victories in the Monte Carlo Rally. Entering the championship would be MINI's significantly larger JCW Countryman, which came with the optional all-wheel-drive facility: just the tool for rallying. Motor-sport experts at the British motor-sport firm Prodrive in Oxfordshire, were chosen to build and prepare the two John Cooper Works cars. The motor-sport preparation company won three drivers' and manufacturers' titles with the likes of rally legend Colin McRae, when it ran Subaru's WRC team between 1990 and 2008. Prodrive is therefore labelled

The arrival of the new MINI brand to championship was a symbolic occasion, marking the brand's return to rallying.
NEWSPRESS

Based on the Countryman, the WRC MINI's direct injection 1.6-litre turbocharged engine has been developed by BMW Motorsport for use in other motor-sport series. NEWSPRESS

as one of the world's largest motor-sport and technology businesses.

In September 2010, BMW MINI launched its first FIA World Rally (WRC) car, in the form of a heavily modified and revamped MINI Countryman, at the Paris Motor Show. In doing so, the car maker also confirmed British rally driver Kris Meeke as a key figure in its driver line-up for the 2011 season. The car would be prepared, run and maintained by Prodrive. Although it is based on the MINI's Countryman, the WRC version features a direct injection, 1.6-litre, turbocharged, in-line 4-cylinder engine, which has since been developed by BMW Motorsport for use in other motor-sport series, including the FIA World Touring Car Championship.

The fact that the MINI name would be returning to the rally stages was music to many motor-sport enthusiasts' ears: but would it live up to the classic that went on to win the famous Monte Carlo Rally three times? The pressure was on. Ian Robertson, BMW AG

board member of sales and marketing, commented on the news: 'The response to our announcement that MINI will return to the world of rallying next year was very positive. The FIA World Rally Championship is the pinnacle of rallying, making it the ideal platform for demonstrating the competitive spirit of our brand.'

Dave Richards, chairman of Prodrive, also commented: 'This project is a truly passionate opportunity. Mini is a cult brand, which left a lasting impression during its previous motor-sport campaigns. We are both extremely happy and proud to be on board as a partner when MINI returns to rallying.'

The Countryman-based S2000 rally car was unveiled in Monaco at the end of the historic Monte Carlo Rally, where former Monte winner Rauno Aaltonen and his BMC teammate and fellow Monte winner Paddy Hopkirk, with the legendary Cooper S, were joined by drivers Kris Meeke and Dani Sordo, who would pilot the modern MINI. Parked together, the vast difference between the two cars is clear to see, and how the iconic small car had evolved into what we'd call a big iconic car.

It was in April 2011 that the MINI WRC team officially presented the MINI John Cooper Works WRC car at MINI Plant Oxford, in preparation to take on the 2012 World Rally Championship. As well as being based on the Countryman production model, the JCW WRC is also powered by the same 1.6-litre turbocharged engine used in the MINI production cars. The only difference is that the engine had been developed by BMW Motorsport to comply with FIA Super S2000 regulations.

The Rally Dakar is the most fascinating rally event on the international motor-sport calendar; its founder was Thierry Sabine, who once described this inspirational rally as 'A challenge for those who go on; a dream for those who stay behind.' Since it all began in 1978, drivers in cars and trucks, on quads and motorcycles, have made their way through the desert to compete in the world's most infamous endurance rally. And yes, the MINI name is once again in the line-up. Up until 2008, the Rally Dakar was held exclusively in Africa and was initially known as the 'Paris-Dakar Rally' due to the location of its start and finish. But over time, these locations have continued to change several times, and what was known as the 'Paris-Dakar Rally' became simply 'Dakar' when the rally began in locations other than Paris. In 2009 the event was moved to southern America, where it has remained ever since.

The X-raid team won the Rally Dakar for the first time in 2012, when eleven-times winner of the rally, Stephane Peterhansel, took the title and claimed his tenth overall victory at the wheel of a MINI ALL4 Racing. In 2013 he returned again to defend his title, taking victory once again in the same car. The Frenchman is the record winner of the endurance rally, and is nicknamed 'Mr Dakar'. In August 2013 he also dominated the Rally dos Sertoes in Brazil, winning eight out of ten legs to finish 1min 49sec ahead of second place. In fact the Rally dos Sertoes is spoken of as one of the most challenging events on the off-road calendar. Taking place on a range of terrain from sand and stones to grassland, it consists of stages up to 319 miles (514km) and a marathon stage of more than 566 miles (911km), of which 404 miles (650km) are timed.

MINI HITS THE CIRCUITS

Looking back, the little Mini was also highly successful on the tarmac circuits, achieving a number of wins in the 1960s and 1970s. It actually became the most outstanding racing car of the entire 1960s decade, with many racing careers starting behind the wheel of a Mini. An example includes Austrian driver Nikolaus Andreas Lauda, known by many today as the one and only Niki Lauda, who entered his first hill-climb race in a classic Mini in 1968 – and he came second. Lauda of course went on to win three Formula One World Championships. Like Lauda, Formula One champions John Surtees, Jackie Stewart, James Hunt and Graham Hill all gained their first racing experiences in classic Minis – and there are many today who still believe that the Mini is the ultimate car in which to get to grips with motor sport.

Since its launch as the MINI Challenge in 2005, this fast-paced form of motorsport has become firmly established as one of the most popular single-make championships in the UK due to its combination of class structure and cost effectiveness. As with any form of Mini or MINI racing, its success is often due to the car's ability to offer drivers 'go-kart handling and feeling'.

The club sport series has become known and loved among many teams and drivers internationally, with races held in Germany, Argentina, Switzerland, Italy and the UK – and what's more, the MINI Challenge is one of the most accessible series, in that fans of Mini or MINI can easily get close to the drivers and teams in the paddock, unlike the politically controlled Formula One World Championship.

The UK championship has twenty races across seven weekends in a season, with eight teams battling it out on track for the championship title. The grid is divided into two classes, the JCW Class and the Cooper Class – this means that fully fledged John Cooper Works cars run on one half of the grid, while Coopers remain on the other half. 2005 was the year the original John Cooper Challenge entered its first year as the MINI Challenge. Between 2006 and 2009, the Cooper S made its way on to the grid, where it would later be followed by the JCW, based on the R56 S, in 2010.

The cars are specially equipped for motor racing, and are assembled centrally by MINI to avoid any

ABOVE: **The Mini Cooper S cars take charge at Silverstone in the 1960s.** NEWSPRESS

LEFT: **An early 1960s Austin Mini preparing to hit the circuit.** ERIC WALKER, SUPPLIED BY GUY LOVERIDGE

forbidden modifications, which could lead to disqualification. Therefore, each class in the series consists of equal and identical technical specifications for all drivers and all teams, making for what the series itself calls 'door-to-door duels in the races' and 'no advantage, no disadvantage, no excuses'. The JCW cars benefit from a performance upgrade in the form of an ECU remap from DNA Tuning, to improve throttle response and provide more torque.

JCW cars are based on the foundations of the turbocharged R56 Cooper S, using exactly the same powertrain found on the standard road cars. The engine is a 1.6-litre, in-line, 4-cylinder unit – similar to that of the MINI WRC car – fitted with a twin scroll turbocharger and direct fuel injection. This block produces 215bhp, but in order to achieve sportier levels of performance on the track, the engine was tuned and optimized accordingly. Its maximum torque of 260Nm is set to deliver between 1,850 and 5,700rpm, making it accessible across the entire rev range. On overboost, this figure increases to 280Nm and a power-to-weight ratio of 5.09kg; the Challenge MINI is actually up at the top of the league table with high performance sports cars.

In 2013 there were more than thirty registered drivers in the MINI Challenge, making it one of the most competitive grids in motor sport. The Cooper Class in particular was at its largest in 2013, and the winner earns themselves a JCW Class drive in the forthcoming season worth more than £16,000, along with other prizes for race winners. What many spectators adore to see is the pedigree Coopers stealing the limelight from the modern turbo machines.

Since its launch in 2005, the MINI Challenge has become firmly established as one of the most popular single-make championships in the UK. NEWSPRESS

FROM THE DRIVER'S SEAT

The inside story with Russ Swift: precision, stunt and *Autotest* driver.

Q: The Russ Swift Mini Display Team was formed in 1981, but you have been involved in motor sport since the early 1970s. After being a co-driver for a number of years, you got behind the wheel in 1972. What was it about the Mini that made it the ultimate racing car?

A: My first six motor-sport events were in a Mini as a co-driver, so I have always had an affinity with them. As I couldn't afford to rally or race, my chosen sport was Autotesting. My first events as a driver were in a VW Beetle, but I soon realized that if I was to get to the top it had to be in a Mini. The reason for its invincibility in Autotesting is its size, handling, precise steering, light weight, low power-to-weight ratio and superb traction, and the availability of a massive range of quality performance enhancements.

Q: Have you always been a Mini owner in terms of road cars, race cars and stunt cars? In your opinion, what makes the Mini/MINI such a desirable car, even now in 2014 following the fiftieth anniversary celebrations of the legendary Cooper S last year? Is it because they're so accessible to everyone?

A: I had been driving for seven years before I bought my first Mini, for the reasons described above. Even to this day, the ultimate Autotest car is a classic Mini. I have always had at least one personal Mini since then. The car I

Russ says the reason behind Mini's invincibility in Autotesting is its size, handling, precise steering, light weight, low power-to-weight ratio and superb traction.

built for Autotesting in 1980 will hopefully be kept for the third generation of Swifts. This car won four national championships for me and an international rally in Sweden before being campaigned by my son with equal success.

I have owned over a hundred Minis over the years, and I still have a 1990 Mini Cooper RSP (Rover Special Products) – it was the first Mini Cooper to be produced after production ceased twenty years earlier, and is chassis number 00001. I first used it in a TV commercial to announce the re-introduction of the Cooper range. I was then asked by Rover to convert it into a cabriolet as they were considering introducing one to the model range. I have previously chopped the roofs off Minis for Autotesting for increased visibility and reduced weight, and adapted the design for a road car. It proved a massive success, and I converted forty-five cars in the mid-eighties, and would have continued to do so if the demand for my displays hadn't been so great.

The car was used in a design exercise at Warwick University to determine the style of the cabriolet eventually to be released by Rover a couple of years later. In the early 1990s, at the end of the exercise, the car was returned to me for display duties. It was eventually offered to me by

(continued overleaf)

Rover, and apart from a brief spell when I sold it to a museum, I have owned it ever since. It has still only completed under 300 miles (480km), most of them on two wheels. I operated a 'Mini Display Team' for Austin Rover and Rover until the end. I performed at twenty-fifth, thirtieth, thirty-fifth and fortieth Mini anniversary festivals, as well as at hundreds of other major events in the UK and Europe.

The Mini appeals to people on so many different levels. It is a brilliant design, has a rich motor-sport heritage, is great fun to drive, has a unique and attractive shape, lends itself easily to personalization, and is still in plentiful supply.

Q: What was the atmosphere like from the crowds when you used to perform stunts in the classic Minis? The Mini is an easy car to throw around, especially at high speeds into corners… is it just as easy to get them up on two wheels? Which of your many stunts is your favourite to perform behind the wheel of a Mini?

A: Audiences love to see me perform in classic Minis. Performing in standard specification vehicles was never easy – 12in wheels made the steering very heavy and compromised stability. A standard spec classic Mini isn't the easiest car to drive on two wheels either, as its low centre of gravity means the balance angle is quite high and the heavy steering requires considerable effort.

My favourite manoeuvre in any car is 'swift parking'. I came up with this manoeuvre in a 1988 'car park' commercial for the Montego. It is my signature move and has been imitated all over the world, and is the manoeuvre that boosted my popularity enormously. It is particularly effective in a Mini. The responsiveness of the Mini enables me to handbrake it to within an inch of a given spot with complete confidence.

Q: Looking at the new MINI, what are your thoughts on BMW's efforts to recreate a classic – in your experience of working with the new car, do you think they have been successful in replicating the original car's handling, personality and characteristics?

A: I think BMW has succeeded in producing a first-class car in the image of the classic Mini. Much of its success must be down to people's affection for the classic. The car's handling is excellent, but due to its size it will never match the manoeuvrability of the original. BMW have drawn on the history of people personalizing their Mini to much success. The classic Mini was designed fifty-five years ago, which is a very long time in the motor industry – think what was being produced fifty-five years before 1959. BMW's Mini is better in almost every area, but only time will tell if it will achieve the exalted classic status of the original.

Q: BMW has certainly managed to maintain the 'Mini spirit', and I'm sure it will be successful long into the future. How many MINIs do you work with at Russ Swift Precision Driving? Do they attract as much attention and admiration from the crowds as the classic? Would you agree that they're just as fun to drive as the classic, just with a little more padding and protection?

A: I have operated the MINI Display Team since its launch to the press and dealers in 2001. I am provided with two new MINI Cooper S models every year: one is used for two wheeling only, the other is used for everything else, and my displays are as popular as ever. Only the diehard classic Mini fans would like to see me still using the original. The BMWs are easier to drive in my displays due to their power steering, and are just as much fun. My concern for the future is the additional technology being introduced with every new model. I was very

Russ Swift becomes the British Autotest Champion in 1983.

pleased to see that the latest model doesn't incorporate a handbrake that is an electric button.

Q: The original Mini won the Monte Carlo Rally three times in four years: 1964, 1965 and 1967. Now the BMW MINI is competing in all forms of motor sport, from the WRC through to the Mini Challenge. Are you pleased to see the new BMW MINI on the race track and clearly achieving great success like its predecessor?

A: It's great to see the BMW MINIs being used extensively in motor sport, though I don't think their rallying involvement will ever emulate the promotional value of the original. The cars used in the sixties were modified but still relevant to the car you could purchase.

Q: What do you think to BMW's approach of producing various different MINI models to expand the MINI range such as the Clubman, Clubvan, Countryman, Paceman and Coupé, which replicate the previous cars of the past? Have you driven all/most of the MINI models, or mainly the hatchback? What do you think to the larger creations, such as the Countryman?

A: BMW is doing a fantastic job of capitalizing on the warmth and affection the public has for anything related to the classic model. It is good commercial sense, and to be expected when a manufacturer buys into an existing brand. I don't have any extensive experience of models other than the Cooper S hatch, but they are, after all, BMWs, and I am sure will be very high quality vehicles in their own right.

Q: Do you think it's fair to say that BMW have produced another legendary car, albeit not quite as small as the original, that will go on to steal many motorists' hearts? Is there anything the new MINI is missing that only the little classic Mini can offer?

A: The BMW MINI has proved to be an enormous success and has a massive following internationally, much greater than the original. There are fantastic events being held for the marque all over the world, and they are giving many people much pleasure, much as the classic did. Long may it continue. It is lovely to see the reverence paid to the classic model by BMW MINI enthusiasts.

The BMW is a very sophisticated, high quality car, but even the introduction models are not cheap. The

Swift says: 'BMW has succeeded in producing a first class car in the image of the classic Mini.' NEWSPRESS

original Mini was aimed at making motoring possible for the masses, an affordable alternative to a motorcycle and sidecar. They are different concepts altogether. In fact it is remarkable that the original Mini went on to be so loved that BMW wanted the brand.

Q: BMW has just unveiled and launched the all-new third generation MINI, which, like the previous generation, will come in MINI One, Cooper, Cooper S and John Cooper Works specifications. What are your thoughts on the manufacturer's next big leap? Have you driven one? In terms of looks and/or driver satisfaction, do you still see a reflection of its predecessor?

A: I took delivery of my first generation model last week. It is obviously a state-of-the-art, very high quality, small(ish) car. I haven't driven it in anger yet, so can't comment on its full potential. It still retains styling cues from the original, as would be expected.

Q: Finally, in your experience with the BMW MINI, what has been your ultimate/favourite adventure? Is there a particular MINI you work with that you've grown very fond of over the years? If yes, what is it and why?

A: My favourite experience with the BMW MINI was performing at the British Motor Show in 2004. I devised a three-car routine, which I performed several times a day with my son Paul. It was the first time live action had been included in the show, and was a massive success.

MINI – THE ONLY WAY IS FORWARD

The incarnation of Britain's beloved small car from 1959 to 2015. NEWSPRESS

Considering how far the MINI has come in fifteen years, BMW has created something of a masterpiece. If it had been left to the decision of top names at Rover, the MINI wouldn't have been or become the car it is today. The designers and engineers at Gaydon were adamant that the 'new Mini' should be as basic and as small as possible. That is not to say that BMW wasn't impressed by the Rover's K-Series powered concept featuring Hydragas suspension, because it was received well and with great respect. But when it came down to the final decision, the team at BMW chose to go for the 'modern MINI', and it's fair to say they probably made the right decision. Issigonis would have despised the Cooper incarnation, because he was the genius behind the twentieth-century Mini

that optimized passenger comfort and maximized interior spacing in the smallest vehicle's wheels.

Although the Mini still firmly holds its place as one of the all-time British favourites, the little car wouldn't have won against modern-day runners. We cherish the Mini for the memories it gave us, its ability to encourage more drivers, the many races it won, and the way it still makes us feel when we drive it. BMW's MINI combines the homely characteristics of the classic and the sporty edge of the original Cooper with the modern-day features of an everyday family car. In fifteen years, having been moulded into a range of MINI creations, the modern hatchback has become more than just a car: it's a way of life, and it won't end here.

BIBLIOGRAPHY

Apostolos, P. 'The Mini Legend – History (Part 1)', *Auto Research 2014* (October 2013)

Adams, K. and Nicholls, I. 'The cars – Mini development history, Part 1' *AR Online* (August 2011)

Adams, K. 'Top 15: Minis through the years', *Honest John Classics* (February 2014)

Adams, K. 'The cars: MINI development history', *AR Online* (July 2011)

Lee, C. *Complete Classic Mini* (MRP Publishing 2003)

Wilkinson, L. 'Mini: a brief history' *The Telegraph* (November 2013)

'Negative Trends in Modern Car Design', *Speed Limit* (March 2005)

INDEX